Earth School

Past Lives and Beyond

By

Gary Markwick

ISBN: 978-1-916732-03-2

Copyright 2023
All rights reserved. No part of this publication may be reproduced, stored in a retrieval system or transmitted in any form or by any means, electronic, mechanical, photocopy, recording or otherwise, without prior written consent of the copyright owner. Nor can it be circulated in any form of binding or cover other than that in which it is published and without similar condition including this condition being imposed on a subsequent purchaser.
The right of Gary Markwick to be identified as the author of this work has been asserted in accordance with the Copyright Designs and Patents Act 1988.
A copy of this book is deposited with the British Library

Published By: -

i2i
PUBLISHING

i2i Publishing. Manchester.
www.i2ipublishing.co.uk

Contents

INTRODUCTION 5
   Why I Wrote Earth School 5
   What the Book is About 6

PART 1 10
   The Kindness of Strangers 12
   Ancient History 26
   A Magical Land! 39
   Past lives - A Journey of Souls 49
   Personal Experiences of Past Life Regression 67

Part 2 77
   This Life and Beyond 77

Chapter 1 79
   An Opportune Meeting 79

Chapter 2 89
   Sent Back From the Dead 89

Chapter 3 100
   Reminder of a Previous Life 100

Chapter 4 110
   Mary and the Potato Famine 110

Chapter 5 122
   The Inter Life 122

Chapter 6 129
   Two More Lives 129

Chapter 7	136
A Last Life Unveiled	136
Chapter 8	141
The Night of the Long Knives	141
Chapter 9	154
Deportation	154
Chapter 10	162
De-humanisation at Ravensbrück	162
Chapter 11	168
The Visitor	168
Chapter 12	176
Pleiades	176
Chapter 13	183
Remembering The Past	183
Chapter 14	194
Rebirth and the Cosmos	194
Chapter 15	198
Cydonia: The Face on Mars	198
Chapter 16	205
Beyond Past Lives and the Anunnaki	205
Chapter 17	210
Cloning	210
Chapter 18	217
Return to Ravensbrück and the Ark	217
Chapter 19	227
Alien Technology	227

Chapter 20 233
    The Gateway 233
Chapter 21 242
    A Creation of Angels and Beings of Pure Consciousness 242
Chapter 22 248
    Earth School 248
Earth School.. 254
    Conclusion 254

INTRODUCTION

Why I Wrote Earth School

It all began on a bright sunny day in London when a client came to see me for a palm reading session. She had travelled from Australia to visit her daughter in the UK. Strangely enough, her maiden name was Markwick, which is the same last name as I have. During the palm reading, I told her that it seemed that she would become quite successful, as a writer of books for children.

After returning home, this client sent an email to me, saying that she had written a book for children and the book was taking off back home. In fact, in due course, she won an award for it. Naturally, I was pleased for her. Then, a short while afterwards, she wrote and said that she had dreamt that I would write a book called Earth School!

I thought about this for a while then realised I always instinctively felt the need to write. I wanted to write about some of my travel adventures, about ancient history, spiritualism, and mysticism, other planets and beings of the Universe. I hoped to combine these themes within a story that included factual knowledge.

In the past, I had written two books, which were similar in some ways. However, they were nothing like the book I was about to write; this was my inspiration and a trigger point towards writing about a journey called Earth School, Past Lives and Beyond.

Reincarnation and past lives have fascinated people worldwide, for centuries. I have been interested in this subject for many years. As a practising hypnotherapist and a Past Life Regressionist, I have regressed many people, some with outstanding results.

What the Book is About

In writing my fourth book, Earth School Past Lives And Beyond, I have been guided by the desire to create a greater awareness of our history, which encompasses the hidden and overlooked. The book begins with an introduction to my travelling exploits around the world. I have included, in the story, some of my discoveries. It contains accounts of my subjects experiences with Past Life-Regression, and continues, and leads on to, a many-faceted and captivating story of one woman's journey experiencing three very different past lives!

During the journey in which Orla travels back through time to the last two centuries, a mysterious character appears. Within these lives, this character has a specific reason to connect with her. At first, she does not acknowledge him but then becomes aware of his presence. After an unexpected approach, this person then explains that he is not from Earth. Eventually, he guides Orla and shows her a past that goes further back to a time of an early civilization on Earth where mysticism played an important role. After this, he shows Orla an ancient history of the world that includes different life forms existing on other planets. She then goes beyond, having a phenomenal experience and witnesses something spectacular throughout the Universe, adding even more meaning to this story.

Within the three past lives of Orla, especially during the third life, she encounters and endures hardship and suffering, which eventually concludes the trilogy. However, during these lives, Orla, also known as Rosa, reaches enlightenment in the third life. She gains greater self-awareness from her experiences and the teachings of her guide. The journey is a beginning towards an end, continuing onwards from the illusions of life on a physical plane to the reality of eternity!

Earth School, recalls an ancient history, which goes back to the third millennium BC, revealing certain truths that lie hidden from humanity. Amongst other things, it also speaks of the ancient Sumerian texts, which are the oldest known forms of writing on Earth. It claims that another civilization or beings, not from this world, either created or genetically modified humans to use as slaves to mine for precious materials.

PART 1

The Kindness of Strangers

Ancient History

A Magical Land

Past lives - A Journey of Souls

Personal Experiences of Past Life Regression

Teotihuacan Pyramids Mexico - photo by G. Markwick

The Kindness of Strangers

Over the years, I have travelled worldwide with my partner Denize and explored some spectacular places, sites and cultures. One of the highlights some years ago was travelling through Central America. We flew from Mexico City to Guatemala and then continued overland through El Salvador, Nicaragua and Costa Rica, finally reaching Panama. These countries were not always safe in the early nineties when civil wars had just ended; it was an adventure of a lifetime.

Within this introduction, I feel it is the right place to share two incredible experiences that I enjoyed during these travels.

The first experience happened during a visit to the ancient pre-Colombian city and the pyramids of Teotihuacan, which are just outside Mexico City. The name Teotihuacan, given by the Aztecs, means the birthplace of the gods. It is where the Aztecs believed the creation of the Universe took place.

Teotihuacan, located in a valley, was the largest city of its kind in the Pre-Colombian Americas. Here, in the

Avenue of the Dead, there are pyramids, including the pyramid of the Moon and the pyramid of the Sun. In the centre of this Avenue, described by some as a long landing strip for certain flying vessels, mounds line the sides and resemble tombs. The Avenue is one hundred and thirty feet wide and three miles long.

During excavation, a 330-foot tunnel was discovered underneath a pyramid. Recently, when a remote-controlled robot was searching one of the chambers that led from the tunnel, hundreds of strange yellow spheres, which were once metallic, were found.

Many people think that these curious objects once shone brilliantly. No one knows why they were used or for what purpose. Perhaps they were there to light the landing path.

It was exciting climbing the steps of one of these pyramids, although afterwards, I did manage to acquire one of the worst sore throats that I ever had. It felt as though I had swallowed a golf ball. Later I learned that it was because Mexico City is the most polluted city on the planet. The situation may have changed since I was there.

However, Mexico City is situated seven thousand feet above sea level, where pollution travels through the air more readily. However, the experience that I had in Teotihuacan could not match that of Tikal.

After leaving Mexico and arriving in Guatemala City, we visited Lake Atitlan, a volcanic lake that, according to some, is the most beautiful lake in the world. It is also the deepest in Central America.

Following this, we planned to take a local bus to reach the tiny island of Flores. We would then return to the mainland to catch a small plane to see the ruins of the ancient city of Tikal, in the rainforest of Northern Guatemala.

The second experience started as we arrived in Flores in the early evening. Flores was also in the midst of the rainforest, and we found that the light aircraft was not leaving for Tikal until the next morning.

At that time, it seemed that Flores was a desolate place. The main reason that anyone went there was to gain access to Tikal. I had no idea where we would stay that night, as there was very little information available.

After the bus left, Denize and I stood with our rucksacks and looked around. There was nothing to see, nobody in sight, only a dirt track ahead and the sea surrounding the island.

This sleepy little town of Flores could be as dangerous as other cities in Central and South America where knife and gunpoint robberies were commonplace. I decided that we should search out some inhabitants. The Sun was starting to descend, and we needed to find accommodation. We were about to start walking when two men pulled up in a jeep. They both spoke in a European accent and asked us where we were heading. They confirmed that it was not safe to hang around there at night.

I asked if there was somewhere that we could stay the night. They replied that it was difficult to find accommodation and so invited us to stay with them. We happily accepted their invitation, rather than spending the night in the middle of nowhere, without hesitation; we scrambled into the back of the jeep.

We drove off; there was hardly a road to follow, and the setting sun dramatically impaired visibility. The driver began to swerve from one side to the other on the narrow dirt track to avoid the rather large potholes in the ground, as the dust created a haze in front of us.

Except for the sound of gravel crunching under the jeep's tyres, the surroundings were quiet. The two men did not speak a word, and neither did we. After a while, it seemed that we had been driving for ages, just following the road around the island. There were no houses or people in sight, only rainforest.

I began to wonder if we had made the right decision by accepting a lift. We did not know who these men were, and as far as I was aware, there were no police officers on the island should we need help.

An hour passed by, we had driven around to the other side of the island, which was even more remote than where we landed. We felt completely cut-off from civilization. By this time, it was dark, without twilight, we were in a confused and slightly panicked state, yet still, no words passed between us.

Suddenly, the jeep skidded slightly along the gravel and came to a halt. Visibility was extremely low! Although, to the left of us, I could see that we had stopped by the edge of the water, and on our right-hand side, I could see a little old house, built with the most basic of materials. Everything was in darkness.

The two men in front got out rather quickly, and we followed. The man on the passenger side spoke, and said, "John will be here soon to pick up your baggage and show you where to stay." They took both of our rucksacks out of the jeep and threw them on to the stony ground.

After this, the two men got back into the jeep and drove off. We were alone in this desolate and unfamiliar place. A little stunned, not knowing what to think or do, but at the same time, trying to stay calm. We stood and waited; five minutes went by and then ten.

I peered into the distance but could only see an open space of land and beyond that, the trees that fronted the rainforest. All I could think about was that I had a small Swiss army knife. I wondered how I would use it.

Twenty minutes had passed; it seemed like hours. Were these our last moments together, or was this an irrational fear based on nothing?

In some circumstances, it is hard to use your intuition. It is better to be calm and relaxed. Perhaps I had used my intuition, after all, subconsciously before we accepted the lift. Could I trust myself, I wondered?

As we waited, I noticed movement ahead of us in the distance; a figure was approaching us from the rainforest. As this person came closer, we noticed it was a tall, well-built man. We could see that he had a dark patch over one of his eyes, tattoos covered his arms, and he carried a large machete around his waist.

Realizing that the Swiss army knife in my pocket was no competition for his machete, we waited apprehensively. Would we need to fight, would we freeze or should we run, or greet him?

He eventually came face to face with us. "Hi, my name is John," he said as he offered his hand. We introduced ourselves nervously.

"I will show you where you can stay and then we can go to the local pub!" Was I hearing him correctly? The local pub? There was nothing around here but jungle, densely populated with trees and animals.

Still suspicious, we followed John into the little old house, where he showed us where we could store our luggage. He then set off on foot, presumably to his *local*, and, unconvinced, we followed.

We walked through the rainforest and then finally came to an opening where there was a small road. I could not believe it. There in front of us was a row of tiny little houses, on either side of the road. These were the homes of the local people. It looked as though many of the dwellings had undergone conversion to small shops.

There amid this oasis, stood the pub!

This pub was located in somebody's small front living room, or at least, just outside with a gate separating it and a counter to sell the beer. John bought two beers, one for himself and one for me, and a soft drink for Denize.

As I stared at the narrow road ahead, I could see nothing but the local men, all with red eyes, crouched on both sides of the road bottles of beer in their hands, many of them vomiting.

I asked John what that was all about. He said, "Yeah! The Indians can't take their drink. One bottle of beer and they are wrecks." We learned about the two men who brought us here. They were Austrian scientists working in the rainforest. John told us a story of how his good friend had been incarcerated in a Turkish prison and was beaten by the guards and then died. They made a film about this called Midnight Express.

John, who was also Austrian, told us that he lived with his mother back home and came here to escape sometimes. It seemed that he took care of things for the scientists when they were in Flores.

That night, we stayed around the table drinking and smoking until the early hours. I went to bed around three am and left them to it, still keeping my Swiss army knife handy under my pillow, just in case!

A lovely elderly lady in an old-fashioned kitchen with a stone oven, cooked breakfast for us the next morning. After breakfast, John called a local native who brought a dugout canoe to paddle us back to the other side of the island. We said our goodbyes only to John, as the others had already gone to work, then headed back across the water.

The scenery was breathtakingly beautiful, and crossing the water was incredibly peaceful. A perceived nightmare had turned into a beautiful experience!

After spending a night in the Guatemalan rainforest in Flores, we took the small aircraft further north to Tikal. After a tiring journey, here too, we spent one night in the rainforest. The next morning, we needed to awake before sunrise, to climb the tallest pyramid in the jungle.

The pyramid was not visible at first. It made me wonder if we were heading in the right direction. Eventually, after seeing what looked like some kind of hill ahead, I began to climb up. I grabbed the earthy bank with my bare hands, occasionally slipping back down as my feet gave way on the embedded stones. At the time, I could think only of being glad that this was not the rainy season!

Tikal Guatemala Mayan Pyramid- photo by G. Markwick

At last, I reached the top of this seemingly colossal mound I thought that I was somewhere near the top of the pyramid, only to find this was the base. There was still quite a lot of climbing to do, seven levels with narrow ledges on each platform.

Eventually, after quite an exhausting climb, I came to an upright steel ladder that led to the top of the pyramid on the final level. As I began to climb this slippery ladder with my camera and lens on my shoulders, I understood one of the reasons why I needed to arrive at the top before sunrise. My hands were starting to get hotter as the sun shone onto them, and I wondered whether I should continue.

During the ascent, someone else climbing on the same ladder above me mentioned that two girls were killed two years before, by trying to wear socks as gloves for protection. Fear crept up as I looked below, I could not see the ground, only what looked like an abyss veiled by mist.

I had climbed over two hundred feet!

Finally, reaching the top, I stood on the narrow edge of the platform of the tallest pyramid in Tikal, staring at the mist. As I looked ahead, the haze cleared, and I witnessed spectacular views over the rainforest. Many more pyramids lay almost hidden in the distance in the thick, dense jungle. In awe, I watched the parrots and other birds flying past.

Ancient History

The Mayan civilization spanned from the 2nd century BC until the 9th century AD, then disappeared without a trace. The fate of its people remains a mystery. Some believe that they migrated to another region. Others think that their original ancestors took them from this world to another planet.

Wherever the Mayans disappeared, I noticed similarities between the local Native Central American people's distinctive facial features. These people claimed to be descendants of the Mayans, support for this comes from the carvings that I had seen on the walls of the ancient Mayan kings' pyramids.

I walked through the local market amongst the decayed ruins, on which volcanic eruptions, earthquakes and civil wars had left their mark. Like the blankets they had woven, there was a magnificent array of colours on the clothes worn by the local men, women and children.

Close to the pyramids of Tikal, there stood a large round stone, approximately four to five feet high and around one foot wide. The stone was used to ground wheat by rolling it back and forth along the ground. However, in the centre of this large and heavy grey stone wheel, there was a carving of a Mayan Emperor, wearing a headdress. The Mayan Emperor appeared to be greeting someone who looked very much like a Chinese man, one similar to those seen in old paintings and sculptures, with his staff, the style of beard and hat he wore. This stone wheel carving dates back to around the 1st century BC. How did this traveller from afar, arrive in the middle of the jungle all those years ago?

Perhaps our history books need to be re-written!

There are inscriptions on the pyramids' walls in Palenque, Mexico that describe a pale-faced man wearing a goatee beard, goggles, or glasses. Goggles and glasses were yet to be invented when this man came across the water to preach love and compassion.

I once spoke to a guide who showed visitors around Tikal who told me that one of the pyramids nearby was precisely half the dimension of those in Giza, Egypt. Some years later, I visited the 'Great Pyramid' in Egypt. I climbed a few of the hefty set individual 2.3 million bricks, which were initially transported, cut and assembled from 5.75 million tons of blocks of stone.

It was not only the size of Giza's pyramids and how they were designed and built with such precision that intrigued me but also the giant statues at the temple of Karnak and the tombs in the Valley of the Kings. How did they work inside these structures without any lighting? As no trace of burning oil lamps on the walls has been found, this is still a mystery today.

Giza Pyramid Egypt - photo by G. Markwick

Many ancient stone-built structures are situated worldwide, some now underwater, and constructed with equal precision. A hair would be difficult to pass through between the blocks. Each built to such high specifications. The stones cut so precisely that one might even wonder if a laser had been used! In one part of the world, the carved stones weigh up to 120 tons per block with six large blocks laid on top of each other.

It has yet to be discovered how these massive stones were transported over long distances. As no quarries, or even water for transportation, may be found in many of the areas. Many ancient monuments of this world are in synchronicity with each other, perhaps in more than one way. They are connecting geometrically with the energy Ley-lines on Earth and the Universe. They have been designed, with religious or spiritual beliefs in mind. It is only recently that these ancient sites were found to be much older than initially thought.

What was their original purpose?

Who built all these great monuments and other ancient constructions throughout the world? Many, like the pyramids, are of similar geometric structure. Was it the slaves and workers of their times? If so, how did the designers, the architects conceive them? Yet, this is still a mystery today!

Perhaps a more advanced civilization or different races instructed them. Is it possible that thousands of years ago beings from another galaxy or galaxies visited us?

The Sumerians, like many other ancient cultures around the world, for centuries, spoke of their knowledge of other planets (only recently discovered) in the solar system and of mathematics, as well as of visitors from other worlds. The Sumerians also had excellent knowledge of an advanced race, looked upon as gods, that came to Earth. They taught humans many skills.

The Sumerian Cuneiform texts, which are the most ancient form of writing from one of the oldest civilizations on Earth, mention a certain advanced race from the stars. They were called the Anunnaki and believed to have created man by mixing their bodies and blood with clay to make the first humans. The Sumerian belief shows similar stories to the Bible and in the Torah, where a God or Gods created man in his image.

Genesis, chapter 1, verse 26, says:

"Let us make man in our image, after our likeness, and let them have dominion over the fish of the sea and over the birds of the heavens and over the livestock and over all the earth and over every creeping thing that creeps on the earth."

The planet Mars has always been of great interest to astronomers and scientists and will continue to be important in the future, in the hope of one day exploring it and possibly inhabiting it. The ancient Egyptians were also aware of Mars through their astronomers dating back to the fifth millennium BCE. Incidentally, the ancient Egyptian word for 'Cairo' is 'Mars'.

In 1976, the Viking 1 spacecraft took a set of photographic images on the surface of Mars in the Northern desert region called Cydonia. The photos were processed in a laboratory and showed, a 2 km (1.2 miles) long mesa (an isolated flat top hill with steep sides), resembling a humanoid face.

Another image, which resembles a face seen thousands of miles away, was similar to the previous structure. In a nearby area, a powerful telescope took pictures of nine pyramids. NASA denied these images and claimed that it was a trick of the light. Equally, they spent a lot of time trying to understand these structures.

Could there be human-made structures created by an intelligent form of life that existed thousands of years ago on Mars? On every continent and various countries on Earth, ancient writings, wall drawings, hieroglyphs, and petroglyphs have been found, dating back tens of thousands of years. They share visions and anecdotes that claim to have had visitations and experiences with beings from other galaxies.

In Kimberley, Australia, there are ancient cave paintings of strange celestial beings that the Aborigines called the 'Wandjina'. They have white skin, large black eyes and are devoid of a mouth showing a halo, or helmet surrounding their heads. The Wandjina had direct contact with the inhabitants of Earth who lived several thousand years ago.

The Dogon tribe of Mali in West Africa say that The Nommos, who were from the star system of Sirius, visited Mali. The Dogon tribe describe the Nommos as an aquatic race that required a watery environment to live in, and refer to them as the 'Masters of the Water'.

Dogon legend claims that the beings descending from the heavens to Earth in a strange-looking boat were half men half women or half fish. Having the upper torso like a human and the lower part of the torso was fish-like with a tail. Coincidently, the Sumerians used the word Dagon for a deity that was half-man, half-fish. The Dogons possessed advanced astronomical knowledge and were aware of the star system Sirius B, which is invisible to the naked eye, long before astronomers discovered it.

The Hopi Native American tribe descended from the Anasazi. They tell stories in their cave art showing the Ant people who had large eyes, bulbous heads, spindly bodies, and 4-6 digit long fingers. They taught and helped their tribe to survive during difficult times on Earth. There is also an ancient petroglyph, a rock carving in Arizona, which shows a dome-shaped saucer.

The Hopis believe that they will ascend to other planets on the day of purification, similar to the second coming's Christian belief. The Hopi name for ant is 'Anu' and the word 'Naki' means friend. The Sumerians connected with the 'Anunnaki' who came from the stars.

Could the beings that visited the Hopis and the Sumerians thousands of years ago be the same?

The ancient Egyptians, the Mayans and the Hopis all focused on the Orion constellation. The Egyptian word Sahu means 'Stars of Orion', and the Hopi word Sohu means, 'Star'.

It seems there have been many similarities between the ancient cultures of this world and their connections to other planets. They share the same principles, symbols, belief structures and religious views. It would seem that this is more than a coincidence!

Symbols resembling snakes have been an essential representation in many cultures and often used to represent creation, rebirth, evil, mother earth, wisdom, immortality, the upper and lower world, connected with the tree of life. These symbols are a metaphor for our DNA!

At some time in the past, we have connected with other beings or a higher power. Is it possible that this higher power has a certain amount of control over our planet and us, giving us a little freedom to make choices in our lives? Still, then we may only be following a path that leads to our destiny because the outcome is predetermined.

Do we know that path before we enter into this world? Could this path be one that we have chosen to learn from, so that we may pay off karma from our past, present and future? As we are the sum of all experiences and thoughts from our history, we are continuously creating changes through our thoughts and actions. Whatever we sow, so shall we reap!

The Universe has created this balance, so that one day we may learn to avoid repeating the same mistakes. As we follow our karma, it may lead us to self–destruction and has done many times in the past. The Universe has also replenished several times, just as Earth did before humanity's presence.

Throughout the ages, stories and written works have shown us how to conduct ourselves and live to benefit our planet and its inhabitants. Then there have been those that lead us astray from our natural state of being, distracting us from our higher selves. For those who may come with good intentions in the future, how long will it take before we can all see the truth of what the enlightened ones have been saying and teaching us for thousands of years?

Many will be in denial, as in the past, and will continue to do so in the future. A child may often understand something of the truth sooner than some adults may, because of their innocence and lack of corruption before entering into a world of temptation.

Unconsciously, our energy can liberate each of us, from believing in lies and false doctrine that has convinced us to live in fear, depression, slavery, confusion and uncertainty.

We need to take responsibility for our lives; otherwise, we may succumb to the negative patterns we may have learned in the past. Many of these negative patterns have come from manipulation and suggestions, often from those in positions of power, usually within specific organizations and often from politics and religions. It has always been the way humans have lived on Earth!

Our weaknesses within and the resulting desires and temptations lead us away from knowing who we are. The more disconnected we become, the more insecure, angry, greedy and power-hungry we are likely to be.

We all have desires, but it is for each of us to know what serves a purpose in our lives and sets us free from limitations. With our hearts closed, we only create negativity and fears of distrust of one another, eventually leading us to destruction.

When we open our hearts and allow a greater awareness to enter; we can share the unconditional love from within and expand it outwards towards others. We then begin to change the frequencies to a higher vibration of energy, giving us the ability to rise above our fears and limitations, as we come to know who we are. If we could all begin to move towards this understanding, then we can change the world.

One may ask, "How can I change the world?"

An answer would be, "first, work on yourself." As we are all reflections of each other, the best way to help others is to create self-awareness in the hope that this will eventually radiate out and inspire those around us!

A Magical Land!

When I was in my early twenties, my long-term partner and I spent six months together in Israel. Her parents had decided that it would be good for her to spend some time on a kibbutz (communal settlement). Having little money, I sold my car, which did not amount to much, and raised enough for the airfare, this left me with around £30, and even though this was not very much, I decided that I would go as well.

Throughout the time that we spent in Israel, we both worked on three kibbutzim. One was very large and modern near Tel Aviv, and the other was in a beautiful setting in the Jordan valley. The third one was basic and situated in the Negev desert with no pure water to drink.

After a while, we decided to move on and hitched a ride to Jerusalem.

Still short of cash, we lived on falafel and had the occasional bowl of delicious vegetable soup once or twice a week, made by Uncle Moustache. He was the owner of a café in the old city, known for his large handlebar moustache.

It was quite strange that when we first arrived in Jerusalem, it was late in the evening and we did not have a clue where to go or where to stay. We had very little money to afford the necessities. Like all cities, they can be a bit daunting when one is unfamiliar with the territory.

However, for some reason, we found ourselves in the orthodox Jewish quarters of Mea Shearim. With few people around, we managed to find someone to ask about where we could stay at a minimal cost. One of the caretakers at a Yeshiva, the Jewish education school that housed the young men and women, asked the Rosh Yeshiva who was the school's head. He permitted us to stay one night. I stayed in the men's quarters, and my partner stayed in the women's section. They did not ask for any money for our stay or sharing breakfast with them. Their unexpected generosity and courtesy moved us.

Fortunately, after a while, I managed to find some work in a restaurant in Jerusalem's old city. There was not much to do except to make Turkish coffee and wash the dishes. Although the pay was minimal, it also included a free meal and all the coffee I could drink.

A few weeks later, by coincidence, I was introduced to someone who was from Colchester, England. This man gave me a job helping to restore a church just outside of the old city, which he would take over and move in as the local Parson.

We stayed in a hostel opposite the entrance to the Damascus gate. I had no problems getting up for work, as the Muslim call to prayer, from the minaret, often woke me in the early hours of the morning. The day started with excitement and full of energy, as we ventured in and around this magical ancient city.

In this old part of Jerusalem, I felt uplifting energy; at times, it was breath taking, especially at sunrise and sunset when all was much quieter than during the rest of the day.

In the early hours of the mornings and late evenings, I could walk in parts of the old city when there was hardly anyone around. It was like going back in time, going back thousands of years. As I walked through the old cobbled stone streets and climbed the narrow steps, which led through the labyrinthine paths of ancient history, I felt moved. I walked past the Western Wall, the sacred site for Jewish prayer with the Temple Mount a beautiful mosque and golden dome situated above it. The Via Dolorosa believed to be where 'Jesus' walked towards the end of his journey stood before me. The Ark of the Covenant thought at one time to lay beneath the temple mount in Jerusalem's old city added to the ambience and mysticism.

The holy city of Jerusalem is one of the oldest cities in our world. It is also a magical land with many problems both past and present. The city has been attacked, captured, recaptured, destroyed and rebuilt.

Throughout the ages, many people have wanted to be a part of Jerusalem City. This city's magnetism and spiritual attractions have been home to the three major religions, Judaism, Christianity, and Islam. Jerusalem's old city is divided into four quarters - the Jewish, Christian, Armenian, and the Muslim quarters.

Each part is of great interest! When walking through the orthodox Jewish quarters of Mea Shearim, women, girls, and public members should respect the neighbourhood. There are signs on the walls of the streets saying:

"To women and girls who pass through our neighbourhood, we beg you with all our hearts. Please do not pass through our neighbourhood in immodest clothes. Modest clothes include closed blouse, with long sleeves, long skirt, no trousers and no tight-fitting clothes."

The religions of these quarters and other places worldwide take their beliefs very seriously, showing great strength of faith. I have witnessed peace and hospitality in many countries, from firm believers in their religions and spiritual practices. However, this can also create separation. When blended with misunderstanding, ignorance and confusion, it can often lead to anger, hate and violence. The only way we can rise above this now is to understand one another, unite and of course, 'forgive'!

Jerusalem is a city alive with people from all over the world, coming to worship and offer prayer, creating powerful energy in the hope that a saviour will come or return to Earth. They believe that this will free them from their sins; this is so in most of the historical and mystical places I have visited. The old city of Jerusalem reached the height of spirituality for me.

Some consider Jerusalem the centre point of the world, particularly with its political and religious issues and predictions about the end of time.

The Book of Revelations speaks of the Messiah returning to Earth and defeating the anti-Christ at the battle of Armageddon. The Second Coming or the Rapture meaning to carry off is also mentioned in the Bible. In Mark 14:62, we have this quote: "I am, and you will see the Son of Man seated at the right hand of Power, and coming with the clouds of heaven." Interestingly, since ancient times in many cultures and religions worldwide, they speak of 'One' or 'they', who will return and descend to Earth from the heavens in a cloud.

Some have described those ascending from Earth into heaven. Others talk of descending in a cloud with fire around them, or beneath their feet. Many have mentioned strange lights from above and a sound heard, described as a horn. There have been flashes like lightning, and a whirlwind, which often appears with a strange vessel, or craft. Beings have also been seen with shimmering light surrounding them and glittering from their bodies or some garment they may be wearing.

These sightings go far back in time, as humans have recorded their experiences by early drawings and writings. From ancient times to the present day, stories abound of biblical prophets and others who disappeared from their homes and Earth. Some have returned several years later.

The prophet Elijah: "Went up by a whirlwind into heaven" 2 Kings 2:1-11. He was seen, ascending in a chariot of fire and with horses of fire. The prophets Enoch and Moses were also taken up. Ezekiel saw a whirlwind from the North; a great cloud with fire flashing forth, and he saw a bright light with glowing metal within the fire. Ezekiel also spoke of four living beings. Mohammed also was taken up when he was in Saudi Arabia at Mecca. A flying horse with wings came and flew him to Jerusalem. After this, a horse took him to heaven to talk with the prophets of the past. Finally, they returned him to Mecca.

Since ancient times to the present, there have been many disappearances. Individuals have gone missing from the planet and groups of people and even ancient civilizations like the Mayans, and others, have disappeared worldwide. Their descendants say that they have returned home!

Strange happenings have always occurred for thousands of years in almost every part of the Earth. Therefore, it may be possible that we were visited in the past and made connections with other advanced beings of the Universes.

What was the original purpose of these beings to visit Earth?

The ancient Sumerian texts tell that the Anunnaki came here mining for certain minerals and used humans as labour. Eventually, they showed us ways to become more civilized and teach us survival skills and other things.

There may have been many beings who have visited our planet, possibly, from different worlds, some with good intentions and others, perhaps not so good. Like many humans of different cultures and religions, who believed in a god, gods, or a messiah, so did these beings. A messiah will come or return to Earth and show us a way to a new age, predicted to appear when there is mass destruction on Earth

Whatever happens, will happen!

Perhaps all is pre-destined to happen in the future, and yet we still have a little freedom to make choices in the present. However, it is now time to change our ways once again, before another lesson is given, to humankind.

We are all still searching for answers within, in the realms of science, religion, and other thought processes; we want to understand more about the Universe. Why are we here, who are we? Where did we come from, did we evolve from apes?

These questions and many others have remained unanswered since we have been able to think and ask them. Perhaps the time has now arrived, when we can know a little more about ourselves.

Past lives - A Journey of Souls

Past Lives Buddha statue - photo by Gary Markwick

For the last decade, part of my work as a therapist has been with Hypnotherapy and Past Life Regression.

During a session before hypnosis occurs, I help the client enter into deep progressive relaxation and then guide them towards their journey into a past life. Of course, it is their journey and their own experience of whatever they may encounter at the time, as I am only the facilitator helping them along the way.

Some clients are not always able to let go and see what might be in their past. It is often due to the fear of losing control or of the unknown. However, this is not necessarily true because the person who may experience a past life is always in control.

Others have allowed themselves to go with the experience and accept. By this, I mean to relax and be open to whatever might be presented to them, no matter how strange or trivial it may seem. When the client begins to trust in this process, they will have an excellent chance to enter a past life. However, it also helps if one can visualize and have a vivid imagination; this is not to say that it all lies within the mind's eye of creativity. It is just that it becomes easier to receive whatever may come towards us when we are open to trusting what is within. We are allowing the subconscious mind to take over from our conscious mind.

The subconscious has a greater capacity to know all things and has an understanding of the higher self. When we access the subconscious, we open ourselves up to an infinite channel. After the session is over, some clients may question their experience and wonder whether it was all their imagination. However, it is usually quite different from something that they may have watched on television or read in a book. The experience of a past life is generally unique to the person who receives it.

A past life experience can be great for curiosity, and some may approach it for this reason. For others, it has helped to free them from their past.

Many adults and numerous children from around the world have had past life experiences. Children, especially between three to six years of age, can recall a past life with less difficulty than an older child may. From around seven, their ability to remember a past life may fade as the conscious mind develops and learns more of the external world. Not every soul is reincarnated and returns to Earth. Some may come to fulfil their purpose only for that one time and then return to a higher spiritual domain. Those who have had an unnatural or violent death are more likely to reincarnate more frequently than those who have not. It may be that when one aspires to both a higher vibration on Earth and a spiritual dimension, reincarnation to Earth may not be so frequent.

The word Moksha known in Hinduism and Buddhism means a release from the cycle of rebirth. In the eastern part of the world, many will live in the hope of completing their life cycle on Earth, freeing themselves from the sufferings of the wheel of karma. An ancient book written in the eighth century shows how Moksha may be achieved; this is done through various steps, which require strong discipline with intense meditation. It can mean relinquishing all that we have become attached to here on Earth. For most of us, this would seem an impossible thing to achieve, reaching such a stage of enlightenment!

Some children and adults who have identified with past lives have birthmarks on particular parts of their bodies, revealing where an incident may have occurred in a previous life. One man who went under regression with a therapist told that he was a soldier in the Crimean War in the mid-nineteenth century. On his return to England, he became depressed and unable to find work. With insufficient funds to live, he committed suicide. In this present life, this man has birthmarks under his chin and one on the top of his head where he shot himself.

Some of these incidents have been investigated and revealed. They are known to be accurate, finding evidence that the person they might have been in the past existed.

Through dreams, regression, meditation, and visions of second sight, people have experienced past lives for centuries. Déjà vu can also often show similar encounters when someone has already experienced a present situation. The person may feel some familiarity with a place that they visit, feeling that they have been there before, or a person may meet someone for the first time and feel they have known them in the past.

We could ask ourselves; perhaps it is not for us to know what we might have been or who we were in a past life. If this is so, why have there been so many revelations worldwide? Regardless of religion or belief, we may hold, others will continue to tell their stories from all cultures and backgrounds in the present and future.

Emperor Constantine, in the fourth century CE, declared Christianity as the state religion. He took over the Christian faith as Patron, supported the church financially, and returned properties previously confiscated. Constantine also allowed the church to be exempt from various taxes, thus creating great wealth. He also had crucifixion abolished and replaced with hanging.

Let us look at the origins of most religions; they reveal a belief in reincarnation and the idea that we will return to Earth in some form or another. In Christianity, reincarnation may have also existed until around the sixth century CE. Then the Emperor Justinian had it removed from the Bible. The reason could have been through fear of losing control of the church at that time, as Christianity was becoming the new State Church of the Roman Empire. In the realms of spirituality and beyond, everything exists. Within the mind or soul, there is no beginning or end because it is eternal.

There have been a few accounts over recent years that I can recall where I have assisted clients with Past Life Regression. One young woman who was about twenty-five; originally came to me for palmistry and ended up having a Past Life Regression session, as many of my clients have done.

As we spoke, it transpired that she was suffering from several phobias during the palmistry session, possibly around ten of them. She had many irrational fears that had continued to build over the years. I suggested that I might be able to help her by using hypnotherapy to deal with these phobias. Later, she came back to me for a session with hypnotherapy, hoping that she might be cured and be able to take back control of her life after all those years. With so many phobias, it can take time and many sessions of desensitization to remove the issues. However, this woman responded well to the suggestive messages that I gave to her. Within two sessions, we managed to cure and eliminate all of her phobias.

Within the time we spent discussing things, I also mentioned past life regression. The client responded by saying she had a strong feeling she had lived before. I did say that some of the phobias present in her life could be associated with a past life. After discussing this further, we then made another appointment for past life Regression.

On the day of the regression therapy, I helped my client to enter into progressive relaxation. I began to use the regression procedure and guided her on a journey going back into the past. I asked her to look down at her feet and notice what she was wearing; this is a standard procedure. However, I often alter this slightly, depending on the client's ability to relax.

Then I asked, "What do you see now?"

"Sandals, with leather straps wrapped around my legs. I am also wearing a long dress; I have long hair and carry a bow with arrows on my shoulder."

It appeared that she had gone back to ancient Greece and was a female Amazon warrior. In this life, opulence showed, as she wore golden bracelets on her arms and around her ankles. The surroundings she described were luxurious, with huge drapes on the walls and a large hall entrance. A mosaic patterned tiled floor and large white marble columns stood beside a bathing pool, which added magnificence and splendour.

We eventually moved on and came to the end of this life, proceeding onwards to another. This life showed that she was a poor female servant during Victorian times, living and working in an old house in Yorkshire, England.

Not a lot was evident about this experience, except that it was a cold atmosphere she lived in, and there was little to comfort her. Only loneliness filled her life.

When I give Past Life Regression, those who can have the experience will often receive up to three past lives during a session. For this client, the following life was where she was a young man during the seventeenth century somewhere in England.

The young man, who was in his mid-twenties, was married and had two children. They lived in a small cottage. He became involved with some unsavoury characters, who had led him astray.

As he left his home one day, the young man carried a bag containing coins on his shoulder, possibly of some value. At the time, he was unaware of two men following him. One of them approached him, holding a heavy object, and hit him on the head. At this point, my client had come to the end of this experience.

I asked, "Where are you now?"

He replied in the voice of the past and said, "Everything is now in darkness."

When death came, he noticed nothing except lying beside a lake, where the two men had thrown his body.

Interestingly, one phobia my client managed to overcome during a session whilst under hypnosis was fear of water, a fear that perhaps has carried on from her past to the present!

Over the years, I have seen clients who have had some interesting past lives. Another woman, who came to see me for Past Life Regression, had two curious lives. The first one went back around two hundred years ago, somewhere in Europe.

In this past life, she was also a woman, looking after two children as a nanny. There was an incident resulting in the murder of the children's father in the house where she worked. Not being able to prove her innocence, she was blamed for the murder and sent to prison.

In another life, around five hundred years ago, she was a man, as an aide-de-camp (an assistant) to a king in

Mexico. The Spanish conquistadors invaded and destroyed the territory by fire, imprisoned the royal families and killed the king. Once again, he, the aide-de-camp, was thrown into prison.

In many of her past lives, the person experienced no opportunity to undergo Past Life Regression to prove her innocence. In the present life, this woman has always felt that no one had ever really listened to her. She also had a feeling of being choked up and found it hard to express herself easily.

These two women's experience with Past Life Regression revealed details of their past which they carried with them to the present time. The revelations brought from the subconscious to their conscious minds have given them the chance to recognize the issues that inhibited them and allowed them to free themselves by finally letting go.

At the end of each life cycle, I guide the client into the inter-life (in Buddhism, known as Bardo, a transitional state). The inter-life is a place, which is in-between lives, leaving one before entering into another. It is where no ego or fear exists, a place of peace, tranquillity and forgiveness. It is somewhere to express your innermost feelings or to say what you might have done differently in the life you have just left, as well as what you may have learned from it.

In her past life, when this client was attacked, leading to her death, she entered into the inter-life. I asked this person what she might have done differently and what she may have learned from that life experience.

She answered, "I believe that I got involved with the wrong people!"

Strangely enough, in this present life, she works for the police as a civilian, dealing with complaints.

The clients who I have regressed over the years have not always experienced lives on Earth. They may have had one past life on Earth, following another experience travelling across the universe, seeing several stars, planets, and often a magical spectrum of electrifying colours. Some have seen shapes of figures in the distance, believing them to be celestial beings. Those who have encountered these kinds of phenomenon, taking them on perhaps a spiritual journey, have said it was like nothing they have ever experienced before in their lives.

A man once came to see me, who talked of feeling a strong connection when he visited the Pyramids at Yucatan in Mexico. He was interested in having Past Life Regression to see what might be revealed. This person was reasonably open-minded and told me that he was not expecting any specific results.

Although this client did experience three so-called past lives, they were very different from what some others may have had, and they were all similar to each of the ones he had. The first experience seemed to flow into the second and the second into the third one. It began by coming out of a forest, which then opened to beautiful scenery stretching out across what looked like a desert and fading into the horizon. Strewn in the distance were large rocks. The colours were unique, a vibrant blue, red, orange, yellow, and pink contrasting and blending with the sky and land.

The difference in what the client saw in these three past lives was that he wasn't sure if he was a beast or a spirit. It was possible that what he felt he was witnessing was in very primitive times, perhaps even before humans existed. After the session, he was quite pleased with how it all went and found it an enlightening experience.

There have been clients who have felt lonely and perhaps a little lost and unhappy in this present life. The reasons have been mainly with relationships, often without having someone in their lives. Some had a partner in the past, and others have never had or met the right person.

There was a case where I regressed one who went back to the times of ancient Egypt. In this past life, they possibly lived affluently, as she happened to be friends with a pharaoh. However, this life was disappointing because she was always hoping for more than just a platonic relationship.

As we passed from this life, entering into the inter-life, I asked how this life had been for her. She replied, "I was lonely in this life."

Returning to the present, although remaining in a trance state, I guided her through a haze, which is part of the process of regression before journeying into the next life. This time, she became a soldier, wounded in the leg whilst fighting for the French Army during the First World War. Once again, she appeared as a lonely soul without a family.

In the third past life, she is a businesswoman who lives in New York in the 1950s. She has a male business partner, and they have worked together for some time. There is a similarity between this one and the first. She knew the Pharaoh in ancient Egypt and the business partner in New York. Both with whom she would like to have had closer relationships but could not make it happen.

After the session, I discussed how she could change her outlook in this present life by using visualization to attract the kind of person she wants to have in her life. It was perhaps time for her to start making new friends and socializing more. I also said that I know it is not always an easy thing to do. However, once you make a start, the world will begin to open up to you!

One day I received an email from a man originally from Vietnam but now living in England. He told me that he had been to see the American Past-Life Regressionist and best-selling author of Many Lives, Many Masters, Dr Brian Weiss. I had been aware of this person and his work for some time. In this email, he stated that Dr Weiss could not regress him for Past Life Regression. He also mentioned that there might not have been enough time to do this, as the session was only for twenty minutes. As well as Dr Weiss, he went to see a woman, who was a reasonably well-known therapist.

This gentleman was very anxious to get results. He said that if I felt confident enough to regress him, he would immediately buy a train ticket and travel to London to see me at my convenience. I felt honoured that this man was ready to travel to London, around two hundred miles from his home, to visit me at such short notice. I replied to him, saying, "It is not a matter of being confident, as I always do my utmost to help professionally." I also mentioned that with Past Life Regression, I facilitated the process, giving guidance and assisting with deep relaxation. What he experienced on his journey would reveal the outcome.

In a way, I was reluctant to work with him, and in a subsequent email, followed by a phone call, I tried to dissuade him from coming to see me. I was hesitant for three main reasons; firstly, he was travelling so far at such short notice, and I tried to avoid any potential disappointment. Secondly, this person was very anxious. The results are often not always satisfactory when one is perplexed.

Finally, most importantly, was that I understood this man's main reason for coming to see me. His wife had died within the last eighteen months, and his godson had sadly passed away. His primary purpose for a visit was to be in contact with them both. I had suggested that a medium would be more suited for making these contacts. However, he had made up his mind, and he was determined to come and visit me. I finally accepted, and we arranged a time that was agreeable to him.

As he arrived, he sat opposite me and began eating the pot-noodles that he had brought with him at a furious rate. I asked him to fill in the usual client forms for hypnotherapy. We talked very briefly, and then we began the session.

I had thought at the time that he would benefit more from a session of hypnotherapy for anxiety rather than past life regression. I have seen quite a few clients ask for this therapy, hoping that they may find answers to their problems in a past life. Often, this can be so. However, I will always say that it is essential to look for a solution to the present. If we can find no reasons why a problem may exist in this life, then we may find an answer in a past life. Of course, there is another good reason for past life regression, and that is curiosity.

We continued with the session. As always, before going into past life regression, I used deep-induction for total relaxation. I also gave ego strengthening by using words for confidence, self-esteem and refreshing the client before waking them to complete the session. When he returned to a fully waking conscious state, he said that he had seen his wife and godson standing in front of him whilst under hypnosis. However, it went no further, without any contact or words spoken.

During our brief conversation, he also told me that he had felt very relaxed, possibly more relaxed than he has ever felt in the past. Even though he did not connect with his wife in conversation, he was quite content with how the session went. Afterwards, he stood up at this stage, said thank you and left to proceed on his long journey home. Most have been successful with their past life experiences, and as long as one has an open mind, the journey will continue.

Personal Experiences of Past Life Regression

Many years ago, at a group meditation in a psychic development circle, I saw myself as a Native American Indian on two separate occasions. I was on a small brown and cream coloured horse, being chased by the US cavalry soldiers. I remember jumping from a reasonable height into a crevasse and landing in the water below. Checking that my horse was fine, I then travelled onwards and continued walking, leading my horse through a valley. The cavalry at this point, as far as I was aware, was not in sight.

There was another time when I was also a Native American Indian. This time I was walking somewhere on the great plains of North America. I passed through a small village that was still smouldering, having been burned down by the US cavalry. Tepees surrounded the village centre, and as far as I could tell, there was no one else around.

As I walked along, I found myself holding on to a rope, which rested upon my shoulder. Looking behind me, I noticed that I was pulling something heavy; a wooden frame made out of a tree's broken branches and formed into a stretcher type bed. There lay either a very old or an injured person on this bed, whom I could not see clearly, as they were covered in blankets. On both accounts of these past life experiences, I seemed to be walking alone as a young man, possibly in my mid-twenties.

When I had experienced these two past lives, it was possibly related to during the mid-nineteenth century when the white settlers took over the lands of the Native Americans. The soldiers removed them from their homelands with catastrophic results. They were taken, often three or four hundred miles away and placed in reservations under US government control to learn to live as white people.

I have had other past life experiences, but these two were quite different, as they were both so vivid and touched my soul. I can still recall them in my mind's eye, just like today. On both occasions, I felt that I had belonged to the Sioux tribe.

Interestingly enough, without having any idea of this, as a child, I played cowboys and Indians with friends; in the courtyard of the apartment block where we lived in London. There was quite a large ball of concrete by the entrance, painted white and situated on top of a four-foot-high wall. As we played, I would choose to be a Native American Indian and sit on this ball, which appeared quite significant to me as a child. I sat on it and felt very proud, declaring that I was Chief Sitting Bull.

In recent years, I had learned that Sitting Bull was a great chief of the Sioux, a nation of peace. He reluctantly went to war, only to fight for his people. However, treaties broke down between the US government, the Sioux, and other tribes. With the land initially pledged to them and gold discovered in the South Dakota hills, the US army disregarded any treaty agreements and invaded their territory. He had a vision about winning a battle and then needing to make decisions with the other tribes, about resisting going onto reservations. Sitting Bull went to war. He claimed victory over The Battle of Little Bighorn, also referred to as Custer's Last Stand. Unfortunately, within five years, almost all of these Native American tribes were confined to the reservations. To this day, the ownership of the Black Hills of Dakota is still unresolved!

Sitting Bull was also a medicine man, a healer and a visionary. Since childhood, I felt some affiliation with Sitting Bull.

There have also been times when I had clients who were mediums and psychics to whom I gave palm readings. They often said that a Native American Indian was standing over me or beside me, and he looked as though he might be a chief!

There was another time when being invited to a house outside London, near Hatfield. A young man from the USA spoke of psychic and spiritual awareness during his European tour, which his agent had organized. After the meeting, he approached me and began to talk to me in a strange language. At first, I needed to adjust my hearing because we had been doing a group meditation. Perhaps I had not quite returned to the entire conscious state of mind.

"Oh, I am sorry," he said. "I thought you were from my tribe, the Lakota Sioux."

I replied, "No, I am from London."

He asked me if I had any connections going back in my family with Native American Indians. I answered him by saying, "Not as far as I know, possibly in a past life."

I also mentioned that it was strange. When I was in my earlier teenage years, I had spent three months in London, Ontario, Canada, staying with my aunt and uncle. They had a caravan where we went for occasional weekends at Lake Huron, not far from an Indian reservation, Kettle Point.

There was a roller skating rink, where kids used to get together, and the Native Americans boys would play. The parents told the other children to stay away from the Native Americans, fearing that they carried knives and would become aggressive. I had no fear, as they were like anybody else as far as I was aware. However, it was there that I was mistaken for being a part of their tribe.

I became good friends with this person I had met in England, and when I flew to San Francisco with my partner Denize, we visited the school, which he ran with his uncle. It was a school for teaching spiritual awareness and healing. He had learned much from his grandfather from South Dakota, from where the Sioux originated.

When writing parts of this book whilst I was in India. I talked with an artist named Salvador, whom I commissioned to paint a picture for the cover of my previous book, 'The Adventures of the Great Marlo and The Blue Pearl'. He told me a personal story and gave me his permission to share it. I feel that it blends in well with the subject of reincarnation. This artist is very creative and an aware and spiritual person, reflecting in his work, so I asked him to paint for me.

Three years ago, Salvador lost his son, who was six years old, due to Dengue Fever. A year after his son's death, Salvador, who was depressed, had been thinking, if only he could receive some sign, to know that his son was okay.

Two months later, after Salvador had sent this thought out to the universe, a man showed up at his small art gallery, which lies next to his house. This man told the artist that his work was excellent and that he was channelling spirits when he painted. Salvador did not respond, as his mind was elsewhere, and then the man said, "I am a medium."

Salvador immediately replied and said that he had been thinking about his son, who had died, and could he help?

The man said, "Yes, I will return in a few days with the answer."

Some days later, the mysterious man returned. He told Salvador that his child was safe and played with other children in a fourth dimension.

When Salvador told me this, I also had a powerful feeling. I channelled the energy and saw his son with his grandfather or great grandfather. Salvador accepted this man's word and believed that he had received the sign he awaited.

Two weeks passed, and one night when all were asleep in the artist's house, Salvador's younger son awoke and sat up. He then spoke out, saying something, which Salvador heard, and that no one else would have said other than the son who had died.

It was the confirmation and was yet another sign that Salvador had been awaiting. Now he knew that all was fine! Salvador also remembers his son saying to him in the past, when he was alive, that he had known his father before.

The father asked in a joking manner and said.

"Were you at my wedding?"

The boy answered, "Yes!"

To date, I have heard of quite a few parents retelling that their children had spoken of different lives that they have lived. A friend's daughter once said, as they were driving along, "I used to live over there, but you were not my mummy then."

I have also heard similar tales from others whom I have known. A client told me that when her daughter was aged between four and five, she ran out of the house, opened the gate, and ran towards the road. The mother frantically screamed out and shouted to her daughter to stop. Her daughter replied.

"Don't you think I know that this is how I died before?"

There are certain things when they are presented to us we may not always be ready to take in and accept at the time. It takes an open mind to acknowledge and know that all things can exist out there, whether we choose to believe or not.

All things must pass! As we move forward in time, we may eventually learn to accept what might be possible and let go of the old ways and beliefs that hold us back and no longer serve a purpose.

In reality, there is nothing new, as it has all existed before, in some form or another. We are only replenishing, renewing and continuing the journey from a past. It is just that we have forgotten!

I leave it open to your belief and imagination as we journey with a story into the past, or perhaps the future!

Part 2

This Life and Beyond

Chapter 1

An Opportune Meeting

Orla was in her mid-forties and had an eccentric character and a wild imagination. She had travelled worldwide and had lived in many different countries, in the Middle East, Africa and the Orient.

Orla had a reasonably strict and traditional way of being brought up with Catholicism. As a child, she attended a convent school back home in Ireland. When Orla was eighteen years old, she moved and began to live a new life in London, which gave her a sense of freedom. She had left much of her past behind her, especially regarding religion and the dogma. Orla felt that she had moved on in her life, although not ignoring certain beliefs and upbringing. Everything holds value and contains knowledge, especially when seen and understood with an open mind and looking beyond the façade of conditioning ignorance.

Having always been a selfless person and having great concern for others well-being, Orla was an experienced nurse. She had been a nurse in some war-torn and poverty-stricken countries, taking care of injured soldiers and working with deprived women and children at the point of starvation. In these countries, Orla had worked as a volunteer and had some experience in counselling.

I first met her when travelling with my partner Denize, on the South West Coast of India, in Kerala. Orla worked as a volunteer in a remote village in Bihar, Northern India, where the people are impoverished. Before working in Bihar, she had worked at Mother Teresa's Foundation in Calcutta at one of the orphanages. After months of exhausting work with dedication and without pay, Orla had decided to take a break and travel.

We were in Fort Cochin, a beautiful part of the larger city of the same name. Here, there are antique shops and tearooms and tiny terraced houses, reminiscent of old English villages, still found in many parts of Great Britain. In this part of Cochin old fort town, there is a place called Jew Town, where there is an ancient Synagogue, dating back to 1568. The Jewish people arrived here in the early 1500s after expulsion from Spain and Portugal. These days there are only around five Jewish Indian families remaining.

We all sat inside the old Synagogue and talked amongst ourselves, admiring the large chandelier above, which covered most of the small Synagogue room. There were beautifully decorated hand-painted tiles on the blue willow pattern floor imported from China in the 18th century, each tile being unique. The atmosphere was peaceful and a little cooler than the intense heat and humidity of thirty-seven degrees centigrade, awaiting us outside.

As time stood still, Orla said, "I don't know why, but I feel a strong connection with this Synagogue."

"Well, it is around five hundred years old," I answered.

"Yes, I know that, but I feel that there is something else, not sure what it is, though," she said.

"Perhaps déjà vu or a past life experience?" I suggested.

"I don't know," she replied.

As we talked, I mentioned that Past Life Regression is among the work that I do.

She said, "I have always been interested in this kind of thing and have experienced going back a couple of times. Once when I was in a group meditation at an Ashram in India, and another time, when someone regressed me into a trance state."

I was a bit surprised when Orla said this, as many nurses that I have met in the past have been logically minded, mainly because of the disciplined work they do. However, looking back, I do seem to recall a few who had been open to exploring the mind and beyond.

She continued to explain.

"It was actually in Calcutta, where I had met an elderly Indian gentleman, whose name was Dr Pramath Chowdhury. He told me that I had had many previous lives, and he could help me reveal some of them. I was intrigued and hesitant; being a little sceptical, not so much because of past life regression, but many will try to extort money from people. Someone I knew introduced him to me, and he lived with his wife and children in a town centre apartment, so I perhaps felt a little safer and agreed to go ahead. As far as I could tell, he seemed to be experienced and had a certain amount of knowledge in this field.

"In the past, I have experienced meditation and entered into states of trance, which led to a past life. So, I thought I would find it easier to relax and allow myself to go wherever it may lead me.

"Dr Chowdhury gave me his address, and I took a bicycle rickshaw to the area where he lived, as it was not far from where I worked at Mother Teresa's. I arrived at the agreed time, around four in the afternoon. It was a small apartment on the third floor of an old grey stone block, in need of a coat of paint, amongst other things, in the heart of Calcutta. It was noisy, as usual, with street sellers, beggars and traffic pollution, and as always, gridlocked.

"There was no lift in the building, so I climbed the stairs, which had a slightly eerie feeling and knocked on the door. Dr Chowdhury's wife opened it and welcomed me, offering refreshments. Dr Chowdhury came forward and greeted me. He was a small, chubby person, with a bushy moustache and glasses, dressed smartly."

"Come this way," he said.

"We walked into his study. I sat down, and he talked a little about his past and professional experiences; we also spoke a little of mine and the reasons why I decided to visit him. Dr Chowdhury then asked me to sit in an old, comfortable leather chair. As I sat down, he produced something from his pocket, a small shiny silver object, which looked like a coin attached to a chain. Dr Chowdhury held the chain between his right index finger and thumb and began to swing it from side to side in front of my eyes. It gave me suggestions for a deepening sensation of mind and body. After feeling a little sleepy, I closed my eyes. He then slowly began to count downwards, guiding me towards an even deeper state of relaxation and into a light trance.

"I had reached a state of peacefulness and went deeply into the subconscious. I was then regressed, going back in time until I reached a past life."

"Dr Chowdhury asked me."

"What do you see? Look down at your feet and tell me what you are wearing, are you male or female?"

"Dr Chowdhury continued to ask the questions, pausing with silence in between. At this point, something changed, and I became a little confused. It was not so much because he asked specific questions about who I was and what I could see in this particular past life. It was more about being in a tranquil and peaceful state. Then, suddenly the path changed into something that I was completely unaware of and a little anxious about.

"I seemed to pass through many lives, perhaps too quickly. My mind, for some reason, was accelerating at an alarming rate, and I could not slow it down. It was like being pulled through a tunnel. At the same time, I was being shown so many things all at once. I couldn't stop wondering what was happening to me.

"So many memories of different lives, without one remaining steady enough to focus. I did not understand what was happening, nor could I see where it was leading. It was very different from a previous experience that I had before, a few years ago, although, admittedly, under other circumstances.

"I was not sure at the time, but at one stage during the session, I thought I saw several creatures, or what may have looked like angelic beings. It was as if they were trying to show me something. They were pointing in a direction that went a long way back and well beyond, to where life may have begun. Possibly, I was not ready for this kind of experience, which is why it went no further as the session ended.

"Dr Chowdhury guided me to a conscious state of mind and brought me back into the present time. He was very kind and asked me how I felt as his wife poured me a fresh cool glass of water. I replied that I was fine, just a little shaky and confused.

"He then said."

"As I told you, there are many past lives that you have experienced."

"I asked him why there were so many at one time and why I saw beings of another kind, and Dr Chowdhury responded."

"It is difficult to say, but it seems that you may have opened up something that is beyond the capacity of the mind for most of us to understand."

"I was a little angry with myself for not allowing the session to carry on. Perhaps this was all about letting go. Could I have been holding on to too much in my life or even previous lives? Maybe this experience became too overwhelming, opening like a floodgate. On the other hand, perhaps I was not quite ready for what was to happen, and there was some hidden meaning that I had not yet discovered.

"Dr Chowdhury spoke again."

"It has to do with letting go and going beyond the fear of the unknown without control and resistance. The mind has limitations. It is all about being able to accept what is, and then transcend the mind."

"Then he asked."

"Has anything unusual ever happened to you in the past?"

"Well, I replied, I have had many experiences in my life, some with near death. When I was a child, I also used to see spirits. Dr Chowdhury responded."

"Often, when certain experiences happen in this life, they may jolt and reveal things from the past, a past life, or even a future one, as all things are connected."

"I thanked Dr Chowdhury for the session. I was still not convinced of the experience I had, as to whether it was all in my imagination or not. I bade him and his wife goodbye and left."

Chapter 2

Sent Back From the Dead

Orla continued to speak openly about her experiences as I listened with great interest.

"Later that day, when I was walking along the road where I stayed at the ashram of Mother Teresa in Calcutta, I recalled a possible reason for this experience. I was involved in an incident and had forgotten to mention this to Dr Chowdhury. Perhaps I had not thought it relevant to our session.

"The incident happened when I was living in Nairobi. The area of the city could be quite dangerous, especially at night time.

"Although I was aware of my surroundings, a man approached me from behind, hitting me on the head. I woke up in the local hospital three days later, with my head wrapped in bandages. They gave me a transfusion as I had lost quite a lot of blood. It took me a while to recover, and I left Africa, believing it was a sign to move on. The robber who attacked me gained little from the robbery, only my purse, with a small amount of money. For a while, after my release from the hospital, I began to have dizzy spells and the occasional blackouts.

"I had always been reasonably logical and a down to earth type of person, but over the days and weeks that passed after the trauma, I began to feel very depressed. This depression went on for a while, and I started to lose the desire to live at one point. One night when I was alone, I believed that the time had come to take my own life. With my previous experience as a nurse, I knew more or less what concoction to prepare for an overdose. I did not want to throw myself off a building or under a car or train. Some would perhaps decide to drink a bottle of hydrochloric acid or take another similar kind of lethal dose. No, that was far too violent a death for me.

"I was to take the easy way out, if ever there was such a thing, by taking enough tranquilisers to put me into a deep sleep forever. So I went to the local pharmacy and bought some pills to do the job.

"I had prepared everything and had written a letter to my few cherished friends that I had worked with at the charity in Calcutta. The small number of possessions that I owned, I assigned to one dear friend and left her a letter. I had also made sure everything was neat and tidy.

"The time had come, and I now felt ready to leave this life behind me. I sat on my bed in the small room and started to take the pills. One by one, with a glass of water, I swallowed them, and gradually I began to feel tired and sleepy. My senses had become numb, and I was losing all sensation in my body. I was without a care or thought for this world as it became distant and began to fade away.

"What a peaceful feeling, I thought, except for one thing, I heard a very faint sound in the distance. I was so disorientated that I had no idea what this sound was or from where it came.

"There was also a light shining through the window that was becoming brighter and brighter. It was a white light, and even though I felt so distant from the world, I could not ignore its presence. As the light became brighter, the sound also became louder. Even though I was non compos mentis at this stage, eventually, I realised that it was a voice. It seemed to be in synchronicity with the light as it became louder and clearer. It was then that the voice spoke to me, saying, 'although your time on Earth may, or may not, be about to reach an end, it is not for you to take your own life. Every life is sacred, and with yours, you still have a destiny.'

"Hearing this, as I was in a state of suspended animation, it felt as though I was drifting into another world with beautiful floating clouds surrounding me. The voice came from a woman; I wondered, was she a spirit or an angel.

"She spoke again, 'Go back; it is not your time now. You will know when it is. You have given to others in this world, now appreciate all that you may receive. Life on Earth is short and transitory and is only a small part of the bigger plan, which is eternity.'

"With these words, it became an awakening for me, and I knew that I had to somehow return to my body. Gradually, I began to force myself to feel my body. By doing this, I managed to move my arm enough to press it against the wooden post of the bed frame, which helped me to regain consciousness sooner.

"Fighting the drug-induced stupor, I eventually rolled off the bed and fell on the floor. I crawled to the bathroom and forced my fingers down my throat, and continued to vomit until I was exhausted.

"I wanted to fall asleep but knew that if I did, I might never wake up again. Eventually, after spending some time, I managed to pull myself up from the ground, and then slowly staggering around the room, I forced myself to walk out into the fresh air. Although feeling very drowsy and sedated, I started coming to my senses.

"As my state of consciousness became more congruent, I started to think. What was I doing, trying to end my life like that? I thought if I were to die naturally tomorrow, then so be it. If I continued to live for an indefinite period, I would accept this.

"Then I remembered the sound, the bright light and the voice that I perceived to be the Angel, who told me to go back, and that it was not for me to take my own life but to appreciate all things in life. I returned to my room, walking with difficulty, doing my best not to fall.

"After that time, I sat for ages thinking of many, many different things. It was as though I was trying to work out why we are here and to understand life and the universe itself. What are we doing here? What is our purpose, if any?

"Eventually, after drinking a lot of water to re-hydrate myself, I fell asleep. As I awoke the next day, it felt as though I had slept for hours. It was two-thirty in the afternoon. I was still feeling a little sleepy, as well as thirsty and hungry.

"It was like waking up to a new life, almost as if I had been re-born. All my thoughts before and after, trying to take my own life, seemed irrelevant now. They had no hold over me whatsoever.

"In a strange way, I felt free, without restrictions of who I was, or what I was capable of doing and achieving. I was ready to accept my life, but with so much more openness than ever before. I still occasionally wonder why we are here and what purpose we serve, if any. Well, that is my story, incredible as it may sound."

Orla laughed at what she had just said and then gazed up towards the large chandelier in the small Synagogue as though she had found peace within. In her eyes, I could see that she was in a hypnotic and almost trance-like state. My intuition told me something was not quite complete in her life, and there was something more to her story.

I wondered why I felt that because Orla had told me that it was like a revelation to her. I was possibly wrong, as we cannot always rely on intuition, even though it has been right for me many times for myself.

"That was an interesting story," I said.

"Yes," said Orla. "It's another story in my life. Before that time, I was married for thirteen years. I was amazed at how the relationship had lasted for so long, and I wonder why I hadn't left before, but now I am free of that. It is in the past," she said.

We conversed for a while and then walked from the Synagogue, through the narrow streets of Jew Town, a name proudly proclaimed on a plaque. Finally, we reached some Chinese fishing nets spread alongside the harbour. These nets are attached to twenty metres of bamboo poles stretching out to the water, with heavy stone blocks to hold them to the ground. Macau's Portuguese settlers introduced the nets, believed to be brought in by the traders from Kublai Khan's days in the 14th century. There has been a spectacular display of an anachronism, which has survived to this day. After watching the sunset beyond the Chinese fishing nets, we walked back to the guesthouse where we were staying.

Kerala Fishing boat - photo by Denize

It just so happened that Orla was staying, not just close by, in Fort Cochin, but two guesthouses away from us. That night, we all went out to eat and, on the way, met a woman from Israel who asked to join us. She was very friendly, and we gladly included her in our group. She was currently living in England but returned to Israel frequently.

When travelling, one meets many people from around the world who have all kinds of tales to tell. There was also an English man staying at our guesthouse. He had been travelling worldwide for twelve years, occasionally returning to the UK for very brief periods to visit friends. He, too, had many stories to tell. Although, after speaking with him, I had wondered what he was searching for, as he often seemed a little confused and disillusioned with life and the world.

The evening was delightful, and we had the best fish we had tasted for a long time. As we all talked, I spoke to Orla a little more about alternative ways of life.

We discussed that we would meet in the future, whether in India or back home in London, as she was planning to move there. We would organise a session for past life regression. I was willing to give Orla past life regression because I believed that she was an intriguing subject, and I might learn something from her.

The next day we all decided to take a beautiful and relaxing eight-hour boat trip on Kerala's backwaters, which was very refreshing. About one week later, Denize and I decided to go south to Varkala's small coastal town. We had stayed there ten years earlier and had fond memories of the place.

Our original plan was to visit the Lakshadweep Islands off the South West Coast of India. They are a northern extension of the Maldives, but it proved difficult and expensive to reach them. The rules had changed recently about where one could stay on the islands. A permit was also required to enter.

Orla had no particular plans and decided that she wanted to join us for the trip. We had no objections.

After a few hours, we arrived by train. Varkala looked a little different now than it did ten years ago when we last visited, which was not surprising, as India was changing fast. It retained its charm with the clifftop restaurants and small shops, although there were many more now. The old Maharaja's house, which stood back from the clifftop edge, had been demolished and replaced with a heliport. For many years, the owners invited people to stay there.

Chapter 3

Reminder of a Previous Life

We found a homestay, where the visitors have their rooms and stay with the families who own the house, quite common in Kerala. In the same homestay house was an Austrian guy; he had been staying there for a while. We began to get to know him, and he later joined us for walks and eating out.

On the second evening, after we had arrived, the woman from Israel turned up at the house with a friend. She had no idea that we would be there, so it was a great surprise to see each other. We exchanged greetings and met in the evening for dinner. The Austrian guy, Carl, Denize, Orla and I, set off earlier and found a nice restaurant on the cliff top with a sea view.

As Denize spoke with Orla, I engaged in a conversation with Carl, a man who was in his fifties and with a reasonably earnest outlook on life. We spoke on different subjects. For some reason, I became curious to know about Austria during the First and Second World Wars. It might well have been because I was in the middle of writing my book and felt that there could be an essential connection with this conversation. I would have been grateful for any information that could help towards its compilation.

I spoke of the Archduke Franz Ferdinand of Austria. He, with his wife, was assassinated in his car, which eventually triggered a series of events that led to the beginning of the First World War.

I also mentioned the uprising of Adolf Hitler, who was born in Austria. I discussed Hitler's political party with him, and the invasions of specific countries and how this led to the Second World War.

I awaited Carl's reply during the conversation, but he said nothing.

Perhaps I was too forward in mentioning the distant past where some may be a little sensitive on the subject, even though it all happened several decades ago. The person I was speaking with was of a different generation. Then suddenly, Carl answered in a deep, quiet voice.

"Do you know what my father did in the Second World War?"

I replied, "No, what did he do?"

"He was a member of the SS."

Not really knowing the details of specific forces that took part in the war, I answered, "Was that the Gestapo?"

Carl said, "No, they were nothing; they were only the police."

I replied and said, "OK, I know, they were the special forces!"

Carl was a likeable kind of character, and recently, we had talked quite a lot about other things. He always spoke in a quiet and calm voice.

"No, much worse," he said. "They took out all the Jews and killed them!"

He expressed this by gripping both of his fists, placing one in front of the other, and then waving them from side to side as if he was holding a machine gun. The conversation had suddenly halted for a few moments, and I became a little speechless.

The Israeli woman had not joined us yet. However, Denize and Orla had stopped their conversation to hear what was said. We all remained silent, not quite knowing how to respond at the time. Then I decided to continue the conversation that I had started.

"Denize is Jewish!" I said.

Carl stared and paused for a moment, answering slowly, and then he responded.

"I'm sorry!"

I detached myself by neutralizing any thoughts or feelings I may have had. As I often do in meditation and then created a positive sense of well-being.

Afterwards, I told myself that his father and not him carried out those atrocities under orders and should not blame the next generation.

"What are your feelings about this?" I asked.

"I never knew really as my father never spoke or talked about it."

"What about the Hitler youth?" I asked.

"Everybody was in it if they were young. My mother tried to run away from the Hitler youth. The main reason was that her father had died, and there was no one there to bury him. So, when she reached his village, she took a shovel, dug the hole and buried him. After that, she returned to her home."

It had seemed, at the time of this conversation that Orla and I were, taken aback, a little more than Denize. It might have been because she wasn't quite sure how to respond. We all show our emotions in various ways and express them at different times. Before the conversation took place, I guess my original thoughts were to ask Carl if he thought that prejudice still existed in Austria after all these years. Many people had been brainwashed by entering into the Hitler Youth in Austria and Germany. However, many would have passed on by now.

The question remained unanswered. Perhaps Carl did not know or would not have wanted to say anyway.

Through the generations and as the year's pass, memories fade, and yet hopefully, not forgetting the atrocities that have taken place in history. In the hope that one day, we may learn from them!

At a distance, Denize saw the woman from Israel and went to meet her to show her where we were. On the way back, Denize mentioned Carl's conversation because it might have been more upsetting for her when she arrived. However, I was amazed how she remained so calm, as if she couldn't care, and was not bothered in any way.

Of course, Israel is a country made up of many nations, and she had probably heard it all before.

Later that evening, when I spoke with Orla, she had expressed how upset she felt about what went on as we sat around the table in the restaurant. It was a feeling that she could not explain. I agreed that I also had felt a little strange from this experience.

Orla said, "No, I feel there is even more than that; it was as though I were experiencing everything whilst he was telling the story."

I answered, "Do you mean it was as though you felt that you were back there in those days, like déjà vu?"

"Yes," she replied.

For curiosity, and perhaps the need to educate and better myself, I decided to read up about who the SS or the Schutzstaffel was. I searched the internet and found that they started as a tiny protection guard unit, as bodyguards for Hitler in the 1920's. It grew under Himmler's leadership to become one of the most powerful and largest organizations in the Third Reich. They were responsible for the vast majority of Nazi war crimes against humanity. They were the leading organization that carried out the holocaust. The SS was given power over all concentration camps. 'Totenkopfverbände', meaning; 'skull unit', was the name used for the SS. Their black cap bore the skull and crossbones.

They also had an oath that consisted of three questions and answers written by Heinrich Himmler.

1. What is your oath?

a) I vow to you, Adolf Hitler, as Führer and Chancellor of the German Reich, loyalty and bravery. I pledge to you and the leaders that you set for me absolute allegiance until death. So help me, God.

2. So, you believe in a God.

b) Yes, I believe in a Lord God.

3. What do you think about a man who doesn't believe in a God?

c) I think he is overbearing, megalomaniac and foolish. He is not one of us.

Himmler based the SS on specific models; like the Knights Templars, the foundation of Jesus, they swore allegiance to The Pope. The Pope's envoys met with Hitler and told him that he was doing an excellent Christian job.

It explained quite a lot to me about who they were, what they stood for and the hypocrisy of it all, how they incorporated God's name, religion, and Pope. Although this is not surprising, many governments do the same when engaging in war by mixing religion with politics.

They convince the people that they are doing the right thing, giving them hope and a belief, fighting for a good cause, and convincing many, they are fighting a holy war.

As with everything, there is always an opposite!

The 'Swastika', an ancient Sanskrit symbol meaning 'good fortune', or 'well-being', has been a symbol used for thousands of years in Hinduism, Buddhism, Jainism and other ancient cultures.

The Nazis took this, turned it around and used it as a symbol of evil.

A couple of days went by, and Orla again spoke of past lives. Previously, I had briefly read her palms, and it had come to my attention that she might be an old soul. The palms of the hands and the eyes of a person can reveal an old soul. It can be when one has had many incarnations and may have lived many lives on Earth.

We decided to continue with a Past Life Regression session, using a room where we were staying. I played some music, which created an ambience. I then used a progressive relaxation technique with Hypnotherapy, inducing a deeper state of trance to ensure that Orla was relaxed so that she may begin the journey into past lives.

She also felt that her previous experience with Past Life Regression back in Calcutta was unfinished and believed there was much more to discover.

After guiding her through the first stages, I asked her what she was experiencing. At first, it seemed that she found it difficult to visualize. I was a little surprised at this because of her previous experiences where everything opened up for her. Finally, Orla began to see something!

Chapter 4

Mary and the Potato Famine

Irish Potato Famine A woman with children - Wikipedia

"What are you seeing?" I asked.

Orla answered in a very calm and quiet voice. "Well, at the moment, it is more like patterns with shapes and colours."

I paused for a while to give her time. It was imperative not to rush things and crucial that Orla's vision comes only from herself and not from my suggestions.

"I can see small white houses built of stone. It is also by the coast; I can see the sea. It is beautiful, the surroundings are so green, and the air very fresh."

"Are you a man or a woman?" I said.

I asked her to look down and to notice what she was wearing on her feet. I often ask clients to identify what they are wearing as it helps to clarify and focus their vision.

"I am not wearing any shoes; I believe that I am a woman," she said.

"Do you know your name?"

"Not sure; I think that it might be Mary, yes it is Mary O' Conner."

As she spoke, her voice began to change slightly, with an Irish accent becoming more apparent. I continued to call her by the name Mary as if we were speaking in the present time.

"What clothes are you wearing, Mary?"

"I am wearing a long greyish-brown skirt and a white blouse."

"And what colour hair do you have?" I asked.

"It is also brown."

"Are you happy?"

"Yes, I think so, although I am not quite sure about something."

"What is it that you are not sure about?"

"I don't know."

"Have a look around you and notice if there is anything that looks familiar to you. It could be people you know or the village, which might be present. Do you live there?"

As Mary answered, a gentle smile came upon her face.

"Yes, it does look familiar."

"Can you see your house, where you live? If so, take a walk towards it."

"Yes, it is over there."

"When you reach it, just let me know."

"I am here!" she said, with a cultivated old-fashioned Irish accent.

"Do you know what age you are, Mary?"

"I think I am around twenty-five years old."

"Now you are at the house, have a look through the windows and notice if there is anyone inside."

"There is a woman with six children sitting down."

"Do you know her?" I asked.

"She is my sister."

"Who are the children?"

"Two are mine, and four are hers."

"Where is your husband?"

"He is out working in the fields, life is hard here, and many are starving, as there is no food. We are all very poor."

Mary spoke in a depressed tone, and tears ran down her face. I lifted her spirit a little and said, "Yes, but you have your children there, don't you?"

Mary answered with a smile and said, "I do."

"Mary, do you know what year this is?"

"I believe it is during the mid-eighteen hundreds, possibly around 1846, before or a little later, not sure."

"What is causing this starvation?" I asked.

"You see, we have been forced down by the British Government. It is the potato famine that is killing everyone, and now all kinds of diseases are spreading."

Mary spoke in an angry but quiet voice.

"What do you mean you have been forced down by the British Government?"

Mary answered, "In the past, under British rule, as Irish Catholics, we have been prohibited from owning any land, from having a good education or even acquiring a profession. Instead, we have been forced to rent small plots of land from British Protestant Landlords who live in England. It has caused the middleman to jump in, renting the land themselves and sub-letting at high prices.

"At one time, here in Ireland, the farmers could grow crops of a variety, but then in England, they began to have a taste for beef. So the Landlords started to use a great deal of land for grazing cattle. There was grain and corn available to grow, but this was mainly exported, leaving the farmers to grow potatoes and to work for next to nothing. Unfortunately, now the potatoes have been blighted. There is no help from the British Government, while many are dying here of starvation and disease.

"I am seeing children looking like skeletons with bones showing and little flesh on their bodies, as their ragged clothes fall from them, for the lack of food. As this goes on, they continue to export the grain and livestock to England. Now many are also emigrating to Canada and America in the hope of a better life. Many say here that it is all a deliberate ploy by the British Government to clear the land of Ireland with starvation and emigration."

After Mary had been speaking, there was silence, so I decided to wait for a short while. I then asked her what was happening in this life and where she was, as some time may have passed, perhaps even years.

Eventually, Mary answered and said, "We are boarding a ship; our families are going to America."

"Do you mean you and your sister's family?" I asked.

"Yes, we are all going to America, New York, I believe," she replied.

I asked, "Who is paying for all of this?"

"The Landlords are."

"The Landlords are, but why are they paying for your passage?"

"Because the Landlords have to pay rates on the land that the tenants occupy. Even if we cannot pay the rent, and no one can because of the famine. It is cheaper for them to evict us, clear the land and send us abroad than to keep us all here, living in our cottages. It has created mass migration, and we have all been evicted and are now travelling to the new world."

"Where are you now, Mary?" I asked after a short pause.

"We are on board a ship with such cramped conditions; there is no air to breathe. Many emigrants are dying from disease and illness; they are too weak to complete the journey. The journey is horrendous, with treacherous weather conditions. We have no light or windows in these quarters; we are on a coffin ship; it is the name that has been given to these ships for emigration."

There was a long silence again, and then Mary spoke.

"We have arrived at the new land. Many are dead, which leaves those that have survived with great sadness and strong feelings of guilt. These were our families, neighbours and the people of our country who have perished. Yet, now I feel that we have been fortunate to survive, and even though I do not know what the future holds for us, I know that somehow we will be alright."

I responded, "That is good, Mary," encouraging her as I spoke, and then I asked, "So where are you now?"

"I am not sure, and everything is fading."

"OK, that's fine, you are doing really well," I said.

As I comforted Mary with words, she had a peaceful look about her and displayed a gentle smile on her face.

I continued. "You are now moving on from this time. You are moving forward from the age of twenty-five and in the future in time, moving ahead to when you are between thirty–five to around forty years old. As you have moved on in time, what do you see now? Look around you and study anything that you may notice."

Mary had no problem with moving forward in time to an older age.

"I think I am in the countryside," she said.

I replied. "Which country are you in?"

"It is America, on the East Coast somewhere."

"Do you have your family with you?"

"Yes," she answered. "The children have grown up and are working. Even though he is older now, my husband is still working, and we have a nice cabin down by a lake. My sister and her children are near me close by. After we arrived in America, life was tough and very difficult for us all. Even before leaving, and only just after we had arrived, there were problems with Irish con men, who were trying to take our last pennies from us. Life has been hard here, but we did have some relatives who were already here, and they helped us a little to get on our feet."

I then asked Mary once again to move forward in time into her old age. "At what age are you now, Mary?"

"I am in my mid-fifties."

"What are you noticing, and how are you feeling within yourself now?"

"I am finding it difficult to move around, and I tire very quickly. I also look after our family's children when I can."

"OK, I would like you to move on ahead, a couple of years from now. What are you seeing, or perhaps hearing?" I asked.

"I do not see anything anymore, as everything is blank."

"It seems that you may have reached the end of this life. Do you know what happened to you in your old age, was it a natural death?"

"Yes, as far as I know, I think I died in my sleep," Mary answered.

"Well, this is one life cycle that you have experienced and have done really well."

I called her Orla and began to bring her back to the present time. However, before doing so, I guided Orla into the haze.

Chapter 5

The Inter Life

I instructed Orla to look ahead and notice a mist in the near distance, a haze. I asked her to walk up to it, telling her that as she does so, she will find herself entering into the mist, a place where she can be safe and secure. Neither judgment nor blame exists. It is on a plateau of a higher vibration and spiritual energy where consolidation and reflection on a previous life can happen. It is also a place of forgiveness, where you may forgive anyone that may have harmed you or you may have hurt and caused some injustice to.

When forgiving others and ourselves, we can move on from where we may have been stuck. It enables us to be free from the past. It does not matter whether it is in this life or previous ones, as we are all the result of our past lives. Here in the 'Inter-life', it is neutral, where only unconditional love exists and where you may learn from your past.

I asked Orla, "What have you learned from this experience, and is there anything that you would have done differently in the life that you have just left?"

She replied, "I don't regret anything, really. It was the life I was given and what I made of it. No, I did what I thought was right at the time. Of course, we all make mistakes in life, and this is how we learn. There were many times when I fought with family and friends, and if there is anyone that I hurt, I would now like to say that I am sorry. Likewise, if anyone has hurt me, I will forgive them now."

"That is good," I said. "Now, I will give you a short time to think of anyone or anything that you might need to forgive or to let go of that no longer serves a purpose. In this way, you may free yourself from any attachments that you have held onto. One way to do this is by sending unconditional love to whomever you may need to forgive.

"Imagine a white light with the colour pink in the centre and then send it out from your heart to this person, healing the past. Now tell them how you feel, and say a few words of forgiveness. Afterwards, say something in the way of forgiving yourself. Perhaps some things were left unsaid before parting, which left you with feelings of guilt, anger and sadness.

"After you have done this, let the colour pink of unconditional love and this beautiful white light of purity emanate from your heart. Allow it to spread and surround your whole body and your aura. Finally, let it radiate outwards, giving yourself the healing that you need. Now, see this energy of light carry on by sending it to your families and friends, then out into the world, healing others and finally the Universe.

"It does not matter whether the other person is living in the present time on Earth; or if they have passed. Unconditional love will find the source, as it knows no boundaries."

Orla acknowledged what I had said by nodding her head as if to say she had done this.

"Okay, Orla, the mist is clearing, and soon, you will see a path ahead, one that will bring you back to a conscious state. Follow this path now, coming back to the present."

I continued to bring Orla to a fully waking state of consciousness into her physical body; I then woke her up. She awoke feeling good about herself and refreshed, although a little sleepy and lethargic as though she had just been on a long journey.

"How are you feeling now?" I asked.

"It is strange, but during that whole past lifetime experience, I felt a powerful presence. It was as if someone was around me," Orla replied.

"What do you mean?" I asked, "Someone like a physical being in the flesh or a spirit?"

"I am not sure, but I know that when I was experiencing that life, it felt real to me."

I said, "Yes, I could see that, as you showed many facial expressions with the occasional tear and smile. I can also feel and often see what one is experiencing during their journey, sometimes before it is even happening. Of course, this is not constant, and these feelings and images come and go. Did you feel that this person, assuming it was a person, was there for your protection or another reason?" I asked.

"No, most definitely, they were there for my protection, watching over me. It is what I felt."

Orla continued further to say, "In fact, now, when I was experiencing this past life, there was a man whom I saw standing in the distance. I think I saw him on more than one occasion."

"Did you know this man?" I asked.

"No, but another strange thing is that even though I didn't seem to recognize him as someone I knew, I did feel that I had seen him somewhere before. If that makes any sense," Orla laughed.

"Mmm," I said. "Perhaps this person is a guardian spirit, sent to watch over you?"

"Yes, I believe that is possible, just like the one who told me to go back when I was in Calcutta that time. I was quite taken aback by that session. Everything was so clear as though it was all happening now, in the present.

Maybe it was the blow to my head that has caused me to open up more on the psychic side," said Orla.

"Yes, possibly," I agreed. "Many things in life have a positive outcome, and everything serves its purpose."

We both laughed ironically.

"Of course," she said, "scepticism did creep in at one time when I was not sure if it was real or just in my mind."

I replied, "You can only know this yourself by using your intuition. If it rings true, then it is real for you! A past life journey is usually different from watching a good film or reading a book that you may be interested in because it is your unique experience and journey. Let me ask you; was it like anything else that you may have experienced in the past?"

"No," she said, "not that I can recall."

I also expressed, "We attract everything in our lives so that we may learn from whatever it might be at the time that we need to learn. It is what you have attracted in this session of a past life that you may learn from, hopefully."

Orla replied, "Yes, I feel that I may have learned quite a lot in many ways."

Chapter 6

Two More Lives

Vads Nurse - Courtesy of Tony Allen post cards

Two days had passed, as we all enjoyed the laid-back atmosphere and beautiful scenery on the coast of Kerala.

However, I gave Orla another session during this time, where she experienced another two previous lives.

One was where she was a servant in a house somewhere in England. There she lived a reasonably happy life, although she saw times of hardship again, but persevered and lived through to old age.

Another past life followed, where Orla was the daughter of a very wealthy businessman during the early part of the last century. In this life, she grew up with everything that one could wish for in a materialistic way. However, deep inside, there was always something missing, and she was never what you would call happy.

Even for the wealthy, this was a strict time with codes of discipline, as the First World War had begun. Before that time, the rich lived luxurious, opulent lives on their estates. Orla's family often gave lavish banquettes, and balls were thrown to entertain the aristocracy on the large family estate in the English countryside.

Her family had previously spent time in America, where the father owned a tobacco plantation. War had changed everything, with most men going to battle, leaving the women back home to do other kinds of work.

Her name, in this life, was Elizabeth, and she had little interest in life. Other than perhaps painting and a passion for being able to help the injured in the terrible war that was taking place. It was against her parents' consent, but after a while, they reluctantly accepted Elizabeth's wishes and allowed her to go and join the VAD, a voluntary service, the Voluntary Aid Detachment. Elizabeth, at first, was given basic cleaning and orderly domestic duties. After a while, she was allowed to assist with the wounded, the sick, and the dying in the hospital. It was there where she met an officer whilst attending to his wounds, they fell in love, and when the war finally ended, they were married. In a way, the war gave Elizabeth a sense of security, enabling her to ground herself.

When we help and take care of others, it can also help us in many ways, focusing less on our issues. These problems will become less critical when we begin to become more altruistic. There is also a sense of achievement and satisfaction, which brings great rewards when we help others.

It was another life that Orla had experienced, a life that brought learning, fulfilment and understanding.

Orla spoke more of her experience as Elizabeth.

"In this life, I was so eager to run off and do what I could to help those in this terrible war. After some first aid and domestic training, I was sent to St Thomas' Hospital in London, where many soldiers were brought.

"Depending on their injuries, some soldiers would have to travel many miles. They were taken in their wounded state, far away from battlefields abroad, before they were admitted to a hospital, somewhere in England.

"The majority of the Voluntary Aid Detachments were middle and upper-class women who wanted to help. Before working as a domestic here, I never knew how to make a cup of tea; the servants always did this. We were told to be courageous, warm-hearted, and bear no grudges but to think of the poor soldiers in pain or dying.

"As I sat with a patient, I saw someone who I thought might be a doctor. I was about to call him to ask about the patient I was attending. Before I could say anything, he came over and said to me, "You are doing fine, don't worry."

"I was feeling anxious and perturbed by what he said as I had little experience in that kind of work. This person then walked up to me and placed his hand on the wounded officer who lay unconscious in the hospital bed. After this happened, I experienced an instant feeling of déjà vu.

"As I took my eyes from the patient and looked up to see who it was in the poorly lit room, he had suddenly disappeared. He was nowhere in sight. Was this the same person I felt may have been around before and watching me in my previous lives? The wounded officer, whom I later married, began to recover very quickly and was then sent to a convalescent home, not so far from where we lived in the English countryside."

"That was a very detailed description of your journey," I said to Orla.

"Yes," she said, "I feel that I am now channelling. It is like seeing it all clairvoyantly. Everything is opening up to me in an obvious way as I experience these past lives. Is it possible that there could be many other such lives?"

"Well," I said, "yes, some believe that we may have even experienced hundreds of previous lives. As with everything, there is a purpose. Our lives lie in the balance of the present. We compensate and re-balance the lives that we have experienced in the past.

"What I mean is, if you have lived a life where you may have been a greedy person, or one who materially hoards things, in the next life, it might be that you could be the opposite. You may stop holding your possessions close to you and start giving a lot away to others.

"Of course, there is always the possibility that one may continue on the same path, repeating the cycle. One life cycle on Earth is only a completion of the physical body and not the eternal self."

Orla answered, "Yes, I see what you mean."

I added that we are all here to learn something. The most important thing is remembering who we are;

otherwise, we will repeat the same mistakes that we make in this world.

Chapter 7

A Last Life Unveiled

The time had come again to move on from Kerala, and after a while, I returned to London. We departed and said our goodbyes to Orla, telling her that we hoped to see her back home sometime. She said that it would be nice to meet up again.

Two years passed since I last saw Orla. I had almost forgotten about her, as I am usually very busy with many clients worldwide. It was not until my partner Denize, and I, went off on our travels again that she reappeared.

We were in Goa, India, where we have frequently visited and stayed over the years. We met her near to where we often stay. I recognised her, sitting in a restaurant. As we approached Orla, she could hardly believe her eyes, seeing us both standing there in front of her. We greeted each other, and I asked her why she had never contacted us?

Orla answered, "I'm sorry, I did go to London for a

while, but found it too much of a rat race and expensive. Now I am living just outside of Bath in the countryside. I always did prefer to be outside the city. I guess that one showed up in the Past Life Regression sessions that we did."

"Yes," I said as we laughed.

She continued, "I even went back to Ireland for a while but became restless and moved around. I have managed to find enough work where I live now to be able to come away and work here in Goa for a few months in the year."

I asked, "What kind of work are you doing?"

Orla replied, "I have been working with charities here."

"We know people who also work with charities," I said.

We discussed the organisations we knew, and then I asked Orla if she was working close by. She said that she had been but was now working down South.

"How long are you here for?" I asked.

"A few weeks, I am visiting friends here and some of

the schools and children I worked with before."

"We must go out to dinner one night before you return," I said.

"Yes," she replied, "I would love to."

"How about tomorrow night; are you free?"

"Yes," she said, "That should be fine. I was supposed to meet someone, but they had to cancel. This was meant to be, wasn't it?"

"Yes, it was," I replied.

The next evening, we met for dinner and talked about when we were in Kerala and other things.

Orla said, "I thought a lot about the sessions of regression that we did, and I always wondered if I was to do another one again, what would come up?"

"One can never know; I have given Past Life Regression to some people who have been very surprised at what has shown up for them. One client, after she experienced life as a Scribe in Medieval England, in another life that followed during the same session, began to see strange figures. These figures were almost in spirit form, white shapes ascending. To the client, this felt similar to being on an escalator. You never know what may be revealed, if you like, and if you have time, we could continue from where we left off."

Orla replied, "You know, I would like to do that. In normal circumstances, I probably wouldn't, but the way the last ones went, I feel that there is still some connection between them. Perhaps something else might come up to do with what has already been shown."

"Okay," I said, "so when shall we go for it? We can use the apartment where we are staying."

"Whenever you like, I have no major plans, and I can always work around meeting everybody," Orla said.

"Tomorrow then," I replied.

"Yes, that will be fine."

"Okay," I responded.

I explained to Orla where we were staying and gave her the address. The following day Orla arrived, looking quite happy to see us.

"You have a nice apartment," she said.

"Thanks, it is peaceful here with coconut trees at the back. They haven't managed to build and obstruct it, like many other places around here."

We had tea and talked a little, and I put on some very relaxing background music. I knew that it would not be a problem for Orla to relax, and as we started, she seemed to go straight into a deeper state of mind. It was just as though she had not had a break from the last time we did the session.

Chapter 8

The Night of the Long Knives

"OK, Orla, where are you now?" I spoke in a gentle voice, knowing that she would communicate immediately with me.

"I am playing somewhere. I think it is a school playground."

I asked Orla, "Are you a boy or a girl?"

"A girl," she replied.

"What is your name?"

"Rosa."

"How old are you, Rosa?"

"I am eleven years old," she spoke in a child-like voice but with some maturity.

"How are you feeling within yourself and the surroundings you are in?" I asked.

"I am not sure. It's OK, I think." Rosa spoke with a different accent from Orla.

I asked her if she knew what country she was in and what year it might be.

"I think I am in Deutschland?"

"Do you mean Germany?"

"Yes," she said.

"What colour is your hair Rosa?"

"It is dark brown."

Rosa began to use some words from the German language.

"Do you know what year it is now?" I asked.

"I believe it is the year of 1933."

"Where are your father and mother, Rosa?"

"My father is a tailor, and my mother works for the Cohn family. They are very wealthy and live in a big house."

I asked, "What city are you in?"

"I am in Berlin. It is where our house is."

From this time onwards, it seemed that there was no need for me to ask too many questions, as Rosa continued to inform me of her life during this period.

"Things are different here now."

"In what way are they different?" I asked.

"I don't know, but they have taken away our books and are going to burn them."

"Who is doing this?"

"The police," she answered. "My parents told me that we have to be very careful."

Rosa didn't have to say much before I realised that she was talking about Nazi Germany.

She continued to describe in detail what was happening in her life.

"Last month, the Nazis stood in front of my father's shop and shouted to the people 'Jude', and then they painted the Magen David, which is the Star of David, on his shopfront window. They also painted it on many other shops in the neighbourhood. As well as posting a sign saying, 'Don't buy from Jews!' It all happened for one day only.

"Many of the Jewish people are now leaving Berlin and Germany. My parents say that we are staying here because my father fought in the last Great War and is proud to be German.

"My mother, who works for the Cohn's, says that they know some of the leaders of the Nazi party who visit them in their big house. Things seem to be changing fast.

"Some Jewish girls have been ridiculed when they are walking past the Nazi youths on the streets. I, and some other girls in my class, are now starting to be bullied by pupils and teachers. They made us come and stand at the front of the class, pointed out our features, measured our noses, and said to the other children that we are different from them.

"My father said that this is a tough time for me, but if I stop going to school, they will know that they have won. He said that we have to try to be strong now, as they are also saying that the Jewish children are lazy and don't want to be bothered to go to school.

"Even on the buses, trains and on all park benches, we have to sit where it is marked 'Only for Jews'. Life is very different for us. I believe it is because of a man named Hitler, who has power and rules over Germany.

"My mother said that we would be OK because my father served in the last war and because she works for the family who knows some people in power. Although recently, something has happened, it has been called 'The Night of the Long Knives', where many officers who opposed Hitler were executed. Time has now moved on, and we have lost our rights as German citizens.

"My mother asked the Cohn family for help, and we are waiting to hear what they say. Meanwhile, my father went to the Gestapo headquarters. He explained that he had fought for them in the last war, but they told him that he is fortunate not to have been taken in for questioning and should not attempt to go there again. We could have paid a fine to leave the country, but something has happened to our family finances that I do not understand.

"We still have some enjoyment at my home with family, relatives and friends who came to my Bat Mitzvah. We also get together for ceremonies and celebrations, as well as every Friday night for Shabbos.

"Back at school, it is not so good. Now Jewish children are not even allowed to play in the same playground with the other children. We are being separated, in every way, in and out of school. However, I still play with my friends in other places and go to their homes where we can also help each other study, as it is becoming challenging to learn at school these days."

As Rosa spoke, she put on a brave face with a smile, but tears would often fall from her eyes and run down her cheeks. She showed her feelings of despair with a complete loss of hope.

"My friend Helga told me the other day that her father, who worked for the government, had been dismissed from his work. So I now feel that we may not have so much luck with my mother asking the Cohn's for help. On the streets here, there is fear in the air and on peoples' faces. It is as though no one trusts anyone anymore.

"I try to smile to others when I pass them by and say 'hello', but it is as if they have hate in their hearts for no reason. Even some of the older people who have known me stare with distrust. I have asked them, 'What have I done to you?' But they turn their heads and walk away."

Rosa became more involved and entered deeper into her previous life in Nazi Germany. She was now sitting at home with her family as she continued to speak.

"What is happening with everybody, Papa?"

Her father replied, "Rosa, the world has simply gone mad, and we are being persecuted for no reason."

"What is to become of us?" Rosa asked.

"I do not know, but we will find a way somehow."

Then Rosa's mother spoke in a calm and assertive voice, "Come now, Rosa, eat your soup, Kneidlach and bread, and do not waste any of it. Food is becoming harder to get now."

Rosa had a younger brother; his name was Benjamin, and he was six years old. Rosa turned to Benjamin, smiled and said, "What do you think, Benjie?"

Benjie just raised his shoulders and said, "Can I go and play now?"

Rosa's grandparents also lived with them in the apartment.

Her grandfather spoke, "I have never seen such times as these, the last war was so terrible and took many lives, but it is very different to what seems to be taking place now. Even our doctor has been told that he is no longer allowed to practice, only as a nurse to Jewish patients."

Rosa continued to explain the situation, "My father has been forced to sell his business by order of the government, and to sell it for a small amount of money. There are no jobs available, and life is becoming harder for us all. It looks as though things are becoming very distressing here. The Cohn family told my mother today that not only could they not help us, but also that they have been asked to leave and give up their beautiful home.

"Fortunately, for them, they have been given documents and papers so that they can leave Germany and travel to Switzerland where they will be safe. Unfortunately, the future is uncertain and unsafe not only for us but for many others.

"It is a strange world that we live in! When I stare out of the window, I can see a blue sky and the trees and flowers with such beauty and colours that would make anyone love to smile and be happy. But, now everywhere else has become dark and overshadowed with fear and hatred."

Rosa paused, looked up and began speaking again, "It is now November 1938, and something very awful is happening. In the early hours of the morning, we are waking up with shouting and the sound of breaking glass. It is happening everywhere.

"I notice that the time is around 1.20 am, and as I look out of the window, I can see the Storm Troopers (SA) and the Hitler Youth. There are others out there, dressed as ordinary people; they are all taking part in destroying our neighbourhood and homes. It has been going on throughout the night. Now it has quietened down.

"The morning has come. Outside our home, it looks as though all is destroyed, and every shop window smashed. Some homes were broken into where innocent people were victimized, attacked and humiliated. Many have also been arrested."

I was amazed at the outstanding description and accuracy that Rosa gave. After this horrific event, many people realised that war might not be so far away. In all of Germany and Austria, over two hundred Synagogues burned down. The night that Rosa had described became known as 'Kristallnacht', the "Night of Broken Glass."

It was a sign of the beginning of many things to come. The Nazis created and used 'Kristallnacht' as an excuse to make the Jews responsible for this incident. They had to pay a fine of the equivalent in 1938 rates of $400 million.

After this, anti-Semitic laws were introduced, which espoused German nationalism to the extreme.

Rosa continued to share and explain her journey into a dark past. "Now thousands are being deported to concentration camps. My family and I have gone into hiding in the attic room above where we live, hoping not to be found by the secret state police, the Gestapo. A neighbour brings us food. She is also living in fear for her life from being caught. Frau Scheinberg is a courageous woman. The other neighbours could quickly speak out and inform the police that we are hiding here. We have heard that even radios have been confiscated from Jews in Germany.

"My father has made the door in the attic look like part of the wall, but we all have to be very careful of any sounds that we make. It is difficult, as we are all so cramped together in this small room. Frau Scheinberg, who brings us food and keeps us up to date with the news, has told us that she knows a local priest of a nearby Church. She says that he has helped hide some children and finds families who will look after them at their own risk. However, Frau Scheinberg has told us that only one child can come. My brother is still young enough to be hidden, blend in with the crowds, and change his identity if necessary, as only adults require identity papers.

"This is a sorrowful moment for us all, as we know that we have no choice in the matter. We want what is best for Benjamin, and if it is a question of his survival, we must make this decision, so we have agreed.

"Two days later, Frau Scheinberg arrived to collect Benjamin. We told Benjamin that this will not be for long and that some friends will take care of him until this is all over. We all tried hard to hide our tears until he left. As we hugged and said our goodbyes, I wondered if I would ever see him again.

"Now, there are five of us left, hiding here. We notice any sounds that may come from outside, in fear of someone discovering us. Other neighbours who live close by cannot all necessarily be trusted. I hope that they will think that we have already left and moved out.

"Frau Scheinberg has returned to us with a secret knock to let us know that it is her. She comforts us a little by saying that Benjamin is now safe and the priest has found a good woman who will take him in. He will leave tomorrow and travel to the countryside just outside Berlin."

Chapter 9

Deportation

Rosa's voice trembled as she described the conditions in which they were living.

"Other apartments have now been sealed off because the people who resided in them have been taken away and deported. We have to be very quiet because the toilet which we use; is on the floor below. We can only use it at certain times of the day, in case anyone should hear us. Frau Scheinberg has told us that all Jewish people are forbidden to use public transport, parks or restaurants. Newspapers are not available to us Jews. It is also almost impossible for Jewish people to obtain any food these days.

"The streets have been quiet for some time, apart from the bombings, which were now happening in Berlin. I wasn't sure what created the greatest fear, being bombed by the British or being exposed to the Nazis. It was all so surreal and different from the past that I once knew.

"Finally, our worst fears have become a reality. During the night, vehicles with soldiers have shown up, and they seem to know exactly where to come. There is shouting and banging going on, and we have all woken in fear. No matter how quiet we may have been, I can hear many heavy footsteps stomping up the stairs towards where we are hiding. My father whispered to me that someone must have said something to turn us in. For a moment, the footsteps stopped, and there was silence, then suddenly, the butt of a rifle came through the false wall. After that, everything happened quickly, with many soldiers and the Gestapo holding guns to our heads.

"So you think that you could escape? No one escapes, least of all Jews," said one of the more minor Nazi officers who had a twisted expression on his face and a bitter tone to his voice, even though he spoke quietly."

Rosa's voice rose as she took a deep breath, "I believe that they are now going to shoot us all, but then something is said amongst them, and the soldiers grabbed us and pulled us and threw us across the room. 'Schnell, Schnell', they shouted out angrily, terrifyingly, and evilly; their voices filled with so much hatred. Then they pushed us down the stairs and threw us out into the road, where we all fell to the ground. My father tried to plead with the Gestapo officer about my grandparents, who were old. Immediately, he was hit and knocked to the ground. Even though we trembled inside, we had to show little fear; otherwise, they would have killed us all instantly.

"We are now being told to get up quickly as they march us to the local square of the town centre. After arriving, I see many other people here as well. As far as I can see, it is mainly Jewish people gathered together in the square, and they are all waiting here for something to happen. There are many soldiers on guard, and they, too, are waiting. As we stand, we try to converse with others to find out what is going on, but the soldiers tell us to be quiet and not speak. We have been in the square for a few hours now, and I wonder what their plans are as we are becoming weary. Then, suddenly, a car pulls up, and there is a discussion amongst the officers. They say that we are moving to a safer place outside of the city and travelling by train in one hour.

"Some people have suitcases with them, and we have only the clothes that we are wearing. However, everyone is told to leave their bags and other belongings in the square. They tell us that the bags will be forwarded to our destination because it is impossible to take the luggage, as there is absolutely no room. All the men here are instructed to remove their hats and overcoats, and the women their fur coats. They are to place them on another pile beside the cases. The time has come, and now we are being moved on. There are screams from some of the women, and the men are shouting. At first, I cannot see why until I realise that all the men are separated from the women and children.

"As the soldiers are separating everyone, I can see Frau Scheinberg, the woman who had helped us by bringing food and keeping us informed of what was going on. Another neighbour who told the police where we were hiding must have spied on her. That poor woman, I cannot imagine what they did to her in the Gestapo headquarters; she was not the kind of person to talk freely. Now it is our turn; the soldiers are coming towards us. As they approach, a young woman screams out, saying that she didn't want to go anywhere. The German officer shouted to her, 'No problem', and then he took his gun out, shot her, and killed her. We are all unable to help anyone, even ourselves.

"They are taking all the men away. We are crying as my grandfather and father are also being taken from us. My father cried out, 'Don't worry, mein liebchen; we will be together again when this war is over.' I have no idea where they are taking us. My grandmother and mother are so devastated, and I can hardly think or believe what is happening. It all seems unreal, as though we are in a horrific dream that has become a worse nightmare.

"The women and children are being directed onward. As we march on, I hear someone say that the men are going to Auschwitz. I am not sure where or what that is, neither does anyone else seem to know. We are all told that we are moving to a better place in the countryside. Some of the older people here have even offered to pay money to ensure that they will have more excellent accommodation with more space. However, I feel that this will be of no use because of how they are treating everyone.

"We are walking to the railway station in Pulitzer Strasse; from there, a train will take us to our destination.

As we arrive, there are many others also waiting. The train is already at the station, and now we are being told to board. There are no luxuries here, with all the carriages generally used for goods and cattle.

As we board, we are tightly squeezed in with other people who are already in the carriage. The soldiers are sliding the doors shut. When the door closes, the fear among us is becoming more apparent. It is very dark here, and it isn't easy to breathe. We are like cattle in a truck, although much worse, because they would have more space. We are sitting and standing almost on top of each other. Fortunately, everyone is very kind, and many people share the small amount of food they have with each other.

"Suddenly, there is a heavy noise of the clanking of chains and a jerk, as we are all thrown to one side, crushing us even more as the train pulls away from the station. It is a slow train, and no one has any idea where we are being taken. Then, finally, after two or three hours of travelling, the train begins to slow down. I can see through the small cracks of the wooden carriage a sign saying 'Fürstenberg'. The train has stopped at the station, the guards slide open the doors and we are told to jump off. It is difficult for the elderly to get down; they all need help. There are so many people, all lost and waiting for what is going to happen.

"The guards are walking past, and each has a fierce dog. Now they are placing us all in a line and preparing us for our next destination, and we are to carry on walking. We are in the countryside now and must have been walking for at least three or four kilometres, some of us are becoming very weary, weak and tired. Eventually, we walk through a forest and come to an open space; with a scenic view. It is a beautiful part of the countryside. I am a little confused about how we have been treated and where we may all be going. Could it be a nice place, and is this the reason why some of the elderly were trying to pay their way to more comfortable accommodation with more space? No, somehow, I do not think so. I can see in the near distance an iron gate, with a high brick wall surrounding it."

Chapter 10

De-humanisation at Ravensbrück

Jude Star - Shuttlestock

Rosa began to speak again. "We are all now approaching the entrance and walking inside. As we enter, suddenly everything is starting to change; I look around and see the wire with spikes above the wall is electrified. I realise that this is not a holiday camp!

"Immediately, the women who are SS guards shout aggressively and hurry us to stand to attention, as they take down our names and inspect us with the officers in charge of registration. We have to place any jewellery that we own in different boxes for rings, bracelets and necklaces. There are many other women here. It seems only women and children. There appear to be thousands; they are all wearing striped clothing with different coloured stars sewn on.

"We are given uniforms and told to change into them, and our clothes are taken away. It seems that most of these clothes do not fit us, being either too big or too small. Now a most unfortunate thing is happening; they are shaving our heads. These women possess beautiful locks of hair - some have very long hair, others are fair-haired, some dark. It is all slowly falling to the ground. Now it is my turn. As they chop through my hair, I cannot help but cry. Others are doing the same as their hair is shaven. They tell us that the hair is put to good use. I see it as dehumanisation. Once cut and shaved to the scalp, all the hair is collected and placed into a large pile. Not all women have had their heads shaved, it seems. Perhaps certain women have been given more privileges than others. I notice that the Scandinavian women all kept their hair. I believe it might be because the Nazis class these women to be closest to the Aryan race.

"After all this has happened, we are all pushed inside the huts or the barracks. It is very crowded here, and we have to share one small bunk between three and four people. These conditions are terrible. The female guards, called 'Aufseherinnen', are also terrible; they are sadistic and want to harm us. An inmate told me to get on and do my work, whatever I have to do, and not look at the guards, even when they call me. This woman said there is one here known as the 'Beast', her real name is Marie Mandle. She waits for someone to stare at her during a roll call, and when they do, they are never seen again. She said this guard is also in control of the flogging. She has half-starved dogs and enjoys sending children to their death. Jews and Gypsies are classed as having the lowest status. The Nazis have just started to conduct medical experiments, mainly on Polish women and the Gypsies. These are horrific, some have died, and others have been maimed and crippled for the rest of their lives. The woman said that two or three years ago here, things were more acceptable.

"All the women who have just arrived are now being ordered to come outside and line up, and we will be told where we are working tomorrow morning. Mother, my grandmother, and I are being given heavy labour, digging roads or working on the land outside the camp. It is because we are Jewish and because we hid in our homes and were caught.

"The next day has begun, I didn't sleep at all last night, not being used to such cramped conditions, and now we are woken up at 4 am, aligned for the roll call. They give us a short time to drink imitation coffee and then go to the Latrines. These latrines serve as communal toilets. Unfortunately, there are only three latrines shared between hundreds of women, all queuing to use them. After this, we are assigned to our work posts and taken to dig the hard ground.

Ravensbrück concentration camp workers - Wikipedia

"The older women are finding this kind of work too hard, and some have already collapsed and died. Only one type of person can walk free from this camp, which is the Jehovah's Witnesses. They may leave, providing they renounce their faith, although it is said that few will do this. The work is very tiring. We are forced to work for twelve hours a day and put under pressure by the guards, who make us do everything quickly. We have a short break for lunch, a bowl of soup, and then we are all rushed back to work.

"Only the fittest and those who are healthy might survive here. Many of the children die, as well as the old and the sick. When we finally finish work, we have soup again for our dinner. Many women secretly make their crafts, things like dolls; these are their most cherished possessions. Some draw and write stories and poetry.

"On Sundays, we are allowed to walk through the campgrounds and socialise with the other women. There are many male guards here, but sexually they do not make demands, as they see us as inferior. The days are passing with torment. There has been an outbreak of fleas and lice, which spread disease. We can only hope for our survival; so much is against us. If the disease does not overcome us, starvation or the SS brutality may. When we can, examine each other's clothes and hair for any infestation. I fear for my grandmother that she will not last long doing the backbreaking laborious work. If she should collapse whilst working, they will take her away, and she may never be seen again..."

Chapter 11

The Visitor

Rosa began to talk again…

"As I am working outside, a male SS officer, dressed in his black uniform with his high shiny polished boots, bearing the skull and cross-bones on his cap, approaches me."

"Come with me," he said in a calm voice.

"I am terrified and dare not look up at him, as this is what we have been ordered to do if and when a guard or officer should speak with us. He tells me to walk in front of him, and my mind begins to fill with fear. I have no idea where he is taking me. Could this be the end of my journey here, and am I going to be terminated? He is telling me to carry on walking. With every step I take, I am becoming more anxious and a little short of breath as I hear the sound of his boots treading into the gravel behind me."

"OK, stop here," he said.

"We have reached a point where it is slightly less populated. I immediately begin to wonder; despite what I have heard about the male guards or officers not making sexual demands on us, there is always this possibility. I know that there are female guards here who make sexual advances on the women here. They entice the women prisoners by offering them specific things to make their lives easier. Some take up this opportunity, but many of the other women here would undoubtedly take revenge if they ever found a girl who had been chosen for these reasons. She would perhaps suffer harsh consequences, often with a thorough beating, from which she may never recover.

"I stand here in shock, wondering if I am to be the first, or one of the very few Jewish girls to be challenged by a male officer in this way. However, I would rather be shot and die before another move is made towards me. As this thought arose, the officer began to walk in front of me, leading a few steps ahead towards the end of the barracks."

"Come this way," he called again.

"Hearing his voice for the second time, I felt that his voice was different from those of other officers; he spoke with a much softer tone. Yet, still, I do not dare to look at him and remain with my head down. Now he is leading me into a gap between two barracks. My heart is beating so fast, and I don't know what to think or do next. I could run, and possibly, he will shoot me in the back. But whatever move I make, I know that I would not escape my fate. Yet, something deep inside was telling me to be still and not to be afraid. I can see that there is a smaller hut at the back of the barracks."

"Follow me," he said as he opened the door to the small hut.

"Even though I had been terrified up to this point, something changed, and I calmed down. Inside the small hut, there are two bench seats with just enough room to sit, as the room has been used to store many things."

"Please sit down; it is OK for you to look up," said the officer.

"I was still anxious, even though a little calmer. Then, gradually and slowly, I raised my head, but my eyes were still slanted downwards to the left. Then, once again, the man spoke."

"It is OK; you can look up at me if you wish."

"I took the courage and slowly looked up towards him. As he sat on the bench opposite me, I noticed that something was different. It was more about the energy which surrounded him, or was it him? The more I looked towards this person, the stronger I felt that something was different here. Suddenly, I noticed a glow around him, lighting up the small room around us. I cannot understand what is happening here. I am wondering in dismay as I begin to look at his face. As soon as I do this, the glowing immediately stops, and I see familiarity in his face. Who is this person? Do I know him, and if so, how? Once again, everything has changed, and my fear has disappeared. Now it seems to have transformed into something magical and powerful."

He said, "You must be very confused right now?"

"As he spoke, I felt the energy between us. Yes, I am," I replied.

"You will not remember, but I have known you in your past."

"When he said this, I became even more confused as to what his intentions were and the reasons why I was here."

"Don't worry," he said. "I am not going to harm you. I am only here to watch over you, although I may not interfere with your future."

"I wondered what he was saying and only knew that my life had become a living hell, far from the happy days that I once had."

"Who are you? I asked in astonishment, and why are you here?"

"I will try to explain as simply as I can, but for now, it is time to return to your barrack before others become suspicious," he replied.

"He stood up and began to lead me to my quarters. I did not speak or ask any more questions as we returned. Back in the cramped conditions, with three of us sharing the small wooden bunk on the ground level, I noticed that my grandmother was not there, and my mother was in tears. Another woman was comforting her. Frantically, I asked what had happened, knowing what the answer would be. My mother replied, 'Your Grandmother has passed away. The work was too much for her, and her heart gave way. She did not suffer; thank God, it was swift.'

"I cried out loud, but deep down, I knew that it was only a matter of time before this would happen. Even the fittest are struggling with these conditions. That night we did not sleep but sat and prayed until the early hours of the morning. It was comforting to know that other women in our barrack wished us long life.

"Despite feeling exhausted and without sleep, we have no choice but to carry out our usual duties to which we have been assigned to on this day. My senses are numb; nothing seems to matter anymore. Yet, we are forced to continue in this god-forsaken, evil place, where I feel that even my soul has left me. I see the same reflections in the dead eyes of the other women. Apart from the little food that we are given, there are only two things that enable them to survive, and these are 'Hope and Belief' for better times to come.

"Three days have passed since my grandmother died. Every night after work has finished, we sit Shiva, a mourning period for seven days. During this time, I cannot stop thinking about my father, who is not with us, but in Auschwitz, I have heard horror stories from women who transferred from there to here.

"On the fourth day, where I am working, the officer or man who approached me before my grandmother passed appears again. Even though I had forgotten about him, it was bizarre that he came to me just before my grandmother died, and now he shows up again. Why is he here, and what does he want from me?"

"Do not say anything, just come with me," he said in an official voice.

"We walk in the same direction as before and eventually arrive at the small hut. I have no fear now; perhaps I may still have remained calm under different circumstances, I don't know. We go inside and sit in the same position as last time. There is no one around;

everyone is working away from this area, although one can never be sure with so many in the campgrounds. I still cannot understand why either of us is here, but decide to stay calm and let this person speak first."

"You are now so curious to know why we are here," he said.

"As he spoke, his voice changed once again, with a more tranquil, softer tone. I am now also beginning to feel calmness and tranquillity coming over me. It is as if I am being guided into a light trance state. 'Yes, I am wondering,' I replied."

"Well, as I said before, I have come here to watch over you and have known you from your past."

"I asked what he meant by that."

"When I say from your past, I do not mean during this lifetime only, but from previous lives that you have lived," he said.

"I was confused; so I asked him what he meant."

Chapter 12

Pleiades

Pleiades - The Seven Sisters - Shuttlestock

Rosa continued speaking.

"As I glanced upon him, his whole appearance seemed to change; he was no longer wearing the Nazi uniform, but a long white garment. He was very tall with blonde-to-reddish hair and large blue eyes. I became more confused at this point and began to question myself.

"I have been so distraught over what has happened in my life; it could be that my conscious mind is shutting down. Perhaps it is doing this to protect me from overload, and my unconscious mind is taking over. Maybe I have become delusional, and I am having a nervous breakdown, unable to distinguish between the illusion and reality, but then, what is reality? All of these thoughts passed through my mind.

"Whatever is happening to me, I must not be seen in this confused state by the Nazis. Otherwise, they will deal with me severely for not being fit enough for work or anything else and prepare me for extermination. So I will decide to go along with what is happening here, to see where it is leading, whatever state of mind I might be in, sane or insane. I don't have much choice in the matter right now!

"Who are you?" I asked.

"I am not of this world," he replied.

"Are you an angel?"

"Some might say so! But no, I am from somewhere very far away from here. I am from the Pleiades; it is part of an open star cluster in the constellation of Taurus. Hundreds of stars exist within the star cluster where I am from. However, the Ancients on Earth know my home as the Seven Sisters.

"The Pleiades are mentioned in your Bible in the book of Job 38:31 ...*Canst thou bind the chains of the Pleiades or loosen the cords of Orion?*

"The Pleiadians have been associated with the fallen angels. However, I can say that there has always been good and bad in every race. This has happened from interbreeding on Earth with humans; and the many generations of offspring produced by our race. It may also be true that some of the Pleiadians are helping the Nazis with particular technology and information! Look ahead now," he said.

"As he said this, he pointed outwardly with his first and middle finger. He pressed his other two fingers against his thumb then swept them from left to right, turning around in a clockwise direction towards the four corners of the hut.

"As I stare, there is a shimmering light, which looks like a whirlpool. It is all most bizarre, and I feel that I am now being drawn towards it like a magnet, being absorbed by its gravitational pull. As I look deeper into its dark centre, the colours surrounding it are becoming so magnificent. I have never seen anything like it before.

"I see shades of an amazing blue changing into a spectrum of colours; red, orange, yellow, green, turquoise, deep blue and violet. Other colours constantly appear every time I close and open my eyes in disbelief. The outer edge, which now looks like a wheel spinning, is white with pink emerging, and in the middle of all this, where it is dense and dark, I can see stars, so many stars. If I am going insane, I can only say that I am enjoying this experience!"

"Look closely now," he said.

"Something incredible began to happen. The Universe opened up before my very eyes, and it was as though I was becoming a part of it all. I was in the middle of a vast unimaginable space beyond time and human comprehension. His voice was beside me, and yet our bodies appeared to be no longer visible."

"Do you see the seven stars, each one shining brightly with blue light surrounding them, over there?"

"Yes," I said.

"This is where I come from; our civilization is much like yours. Yet, we are a more advanced civilization, as you will be in the far distant future from now. You can see by looking into the Universe there are so many stars. In your galaxy alone, there are as many as four hundred billion planets. There are as many stars in the Universe as there are grains of sands on this planet you call Earth."

"As he spoke, I was lost for words and continued to wonder whether I was here or there?"

"Don't worry, you are safe here," he said.

"I felt safe, and somehow the fears, which had existed until now, left me. Then suddenly, something changed, and I was back in the hut, sitting opposite this extra-terrestrial being, who turned to me and spoke quietly."

"It is time for you to return to your barracks now."

"As I returned to where we all slept, it was as if I had not been away, as no one questioned me at all. I began to speak to my mother about some of the things that had happened to me. She told me not to be so crazy. If anyone heard of such things, we would be reported, taken away and executed. From this time onwards, I must keep all of this a secret, as no one is ever going to believe me.

"Am I going crazy? This whole place appears like hell, and I am sure many others would describe it as such. It is enough to drive anyone to insanity, and it is doing just that every day to someone. How can we know what is the reality here? The only thing that keeps us a little sane is talking to one another and the arduous work. Being able to feel the pain in our bodies from working long hours, helps keep us grounded.

"Two years have passed since we arrived here, and it is becoming much more challenging to survive. Many of us are dying every day from disease, starvation and exhaustion, as well as executions. We live in the hope that soon, either the British or the Americans will rescue us. I worry a lot about my mother, as she has become very frail, and she still has to work, as we all do.

"Once again, this person from another planet has contacted me. I am no longer surprised that he should approach me at any time because he can communicate with me through telepathy. After receiving his message, I go with him, when possible, to the same hut as before. One time I told him that I still did not understand why he was here, and he replied."

"Call it a case study if you like. We can learn much from humans and their behaviour, even though we are an advanced civilization compared to yours, still in primitive stages. Let me help you see some of your previous lives."

Chapter 13

Remembering The Past

Crystal Children - photo by D Churnin

Rosa began to speak again.

"As he places his hand on my head, I can see many shapes. At first, I do not recognize what they are. Slowly, they appear as figures of people and then faces. I can see their clothes and the costumes they are wearing. There are many people, old and young, children as well. Buildings, animals, plants and other things are shown to me. It is as though I am living in these different times. There are so many of them, going back centuries, even thousands of years of varying cultures and countries."

"You have lived many lives," he said.

"Now I can see him standing beside me in another place and another time. Then it began to happen repeatedly, again, and again, and again past lives were revealed with him standing close by me. It is coming back to me.

"I remember you. Yes," I said. "I do remember you! Have you always been there? I asked, and he replied."

"Not always, but on many occasions. Time is an illusion; it is the same, past, present and future. Through other dimensions, we can travel and visit planets like Earth. We have been here for more than two hundred and twenty-five thousand Earth years; many of us came here from our civilization and stayed a long time. After teaching you skills and knowledge, we left. Some of us have returned to pursue specific interests and to monitor any progress humans may have made.

"We are communicating with many of you and are helping to raise your consciousness here on Earth. So it will continue with future generations, and aware children will be born and known to you as Crystal, Indigo, Star and Rainbow Children. These children will go beyond the understanding of ordinary people governed by ego and fear on Earth.

"Most people have forgotten who they are, but these special children will remember. They will listen within, using their inner senses, going beyond intellect and even normal psychic abilities. They will connect and travel to other worlds at night time when they sleep. They will receive messages that will guide them towards showing and helping others on Earth to create a new world that all may benefit from. However, there will always be those who resist the changes.

"There have been other galactic beings who visited Earth before. Some have not been so helpful and kind to the human race. They have taken many shapes and forms. Some of those who have travelled here are from other constellations and the planets of Mars, Orion and Sirius. The Pleiades have contributed to your advancement. Different beings inhabit many worlds. You also have a great variety of creatures that live on land and in the sea, different from human beings.

"Many creatures live below the Earth's surface. These creatures are half-human and half-animal, known as the 'Mazikim'. Your people may know them as the fallen angels, the demons. Not all of these are in physical form, as some are non-physical entities or spirits. You see me now how I am, and how I look when I am with my people. It is not so different from many humans, especially the Nordic or Northern European races on Earth. Of course, we speak in another tongue or language, as you may say, and dress a little differently, but there are many similarities.

"There have been many wars between other beings from different worlds, and there have been many rulers. One who rules over your dominion in the universe has now left you to make your own choices. However, they will return eventually. It will happen before humans destroy themselves irrevocably.

"Humans have reached a point of destruction several times in the past. However, there will always be many who fight for the good. At times, there will be peace on Earth, but because of those who strive for control and power; it will eventually lead towards the mass destruction of your planet."

"He finished speaking, and I realised that I had been listening intently. It was difficult for me to comprehend and take it all in. Strangely, it seemed to make sense looking at the world in its present state and the suffering we all endure. Perhaps it has always been this way. I began to wonder as he started to speak again."

"Many of you will place the blame on others," he said in a calm voice whilst making a peaceful gesture with his hands, "or you will say that if there is a God, why would he let all this happen? But, it is of your doing that has contributed towards your destruction."

"Yes, I can see this, I believe that the world was beautiful before, and now it has changed. I replied."

"The World, or should I say the Earth, always has and will continue to appear to many, as a beautiful place. Your planet Earth is one of the few in the entire galaxy that has such beauty.

"I asked him how this can be seen as a beautiful world to inhabit in the future. Why would anyone think it is beautiful if you look at what is happening now with two world wars so close to one another? He could see how upset I was becoming."

"This war will pass, and there will be no more wars for some time. However, there will always be wars and threats; some will be small and others great. Eventually, this will lead to one conflict, which will affect everyone on the planet. It is inevitable; wars are inevitable."

"Once again, I asked, when will this war end, and he answered straight away."

"That I cannot tell you just yet; I will let you know something about it soon. Now it is time for you to return to the barracks. On my next visit, I will show you how it all began, and you will have a greater understanding of what I have said. We will walk back now; no one will see you until you are inside with the others."

"I answered him with scepticism and asked him how this was possible."

"Let's just say, it is a manipulation of the speed of light, in which you become invisible to others who are around you."

"I am curious to see what is going to happen. Suddenly, there is a flash of light, and although I do not see or feel any different, the guards at their posts cannot see me. As I entered the barracks, I became visible, and as the room was so crowded, no one noticed my absence.

"I did not know when I would see this man again. Before we parted, he told me that his name was Aleaze. His appearance was similar to that of some of the Nazis; he was tall with blonde hair and bluish-grey eyes. He was like someone that Hitler would wish all the men to look like in the future, the Aryan race. Yet, even though there are similarities with his looks, some of his facial features are a bit different. His body shape is also more slender, and he wears his hair longer than the others do. I still wonder why Aleaze has chosen me to visit; there are so many of us here.

"The days in the camp are becoming harder for most of us, as starvation and disease increases. Now a doctor comes along, with the commandant, once a week to inspect us. They tell each woman to run up and down straight and raise their skirts to the hips. We will pass the test without problems if our hips, legs, ankles, or feet are strong. If we fail, they will select us; then take us to a hut where the sick lay and left to die. No one ever comes out after entering this hut. No food is given to anyone either. The most crucial policy in the camp here is to work and then to die.

"It is strange or perhaps not so strange that as my flesh becomes weaker, I feel my spirit becoming stronger every day. I can continue with the arduous work here because I can detach myself from my body. I now know that I am more than just my body; the higher power works within me, the doer. However, I am worried about my mother. She has become weaker through the lack of food and the hard work, and she may not last much longer. It is only a matter of time. The winters also take the lives of weak ones, and some summers, which can be so hot, the weak collapse with thirst, hunger, and exhaustion. As I worry about my mother, Aleaze appears to me in a vision, and we meet again at the same place. He starts to speak."

"One of the reasons I have been coming here to see you, here and in your past, is because you are a descendant of a certain tribe that goes back to ancient times on Earth. So I will show you some things, which go a long way back in time."

"I interrupted with anger and called out to ask him, what is the use and meaning of all of this? We are not concerned or interested in any of this. We are all dying here of many different diseases and illnesses, of starvation, experiments and torture. My mother is going to die any time now. I am feeling that even though there are times when I can separate from my physical self to detach from the many things that are happening here, it is often too much to bear. No one could do such a thing under these circumstances.

"There was a silence as he stared at me, and I looked straight ahead with a feeling of emptiness inside of me. Then, in a calm and tranquil way, he spoke again."

"I know that it is most challenging here and almost impossible to bear these conditions of severe hardship and suffering, but you must still have faith. I will give you some basic food to help a little. This goes against the instructions from my superiors of the Galactic Federation where I am from."

"Aleaze reached his hand out."

"Please take these two small round purple pills," he said.

"I asked him what they were, as they did not seem big enough to feed an insect."

"There are substantial ingredients and nutrients within each pill to give you what you need for a short time, but not for more than four days," he said.

"Once again, I glared at him with scepticism, but I took the pills and hid them on my body in case the guards searched me."

Chapter 14

Rebirth and the Cosmos

The Cosmos - photo by D Churnin

Rosa continued.

"Aleaze asked if it was okay to show me something. I had calmed down a little by then and answered in the affirmative. As I continued to stare ahead, sitting in the middle of the small hut, everything suddenly became dark around me. Then it was as if the Universe once again began to open up, and I became a part of it all. Aleaze spoke to me."

"The Universe has been reborn many times with continuous cycles of birth and death through fire. Now I would like you to let go and experience whatever may come to you, as this is your journey."

"I took his advice and 'let go'. I found myself going beyond the darkness and into the light. A white light, a flash, was beginning to expand with millions of coloured shapes and stars. Is this how it all began, or is there a beginning? I am now in another place or time. Yet, there is no time. It does not exist here, and perhaps it is another dimension or multidimensional, I don't know? There are other worlds, and now I can see that there are other beings around me. They seem to be neither male nor female. I am experiencing peace and serenity with beauty. Here, there is nothing but peace, love, and harmony. It is as if I have come back home, but not on planet Earth.

"Here, it is so beautiful, and everything is as it always was and always will be. I can also see other universes, planets and worlds that exist out there within the different dimensions of space. All life arises from pre-existing life, which goes back to the origins of the Universe. Yet, it seems that there is no beginning or end. It just is; it is eternal! Now I understand that there is no death. Life goes on.

"I can hear a voice speaking to me, although I am not sure if it is Aleaze's voice, as it is a little distant. It tells me that, 'to find liberation from this world; it is as if one has to pass through a hole in the Universe. If there is success in passing through, then one becomes free from the cycles of life and death. Those who do not pass through are reborn and return to Earth. Very few will pass through to the higher dimensions. Only those who have renounced all possessions and detached from worldly pleasures will go through. Letting go of attachments will free them from the Karmic cycle, repeated during many lifetimes on Earth. For most, as long as there is hatred, blame, anger, greed, possessiveness and jealousy, rebirth will continue. All these emotions are lower energy vibrations. All humans must eventually learn to go beyond them! The energy of negativity or dark forces will also continue. It will always work its way into the hearts of those who are open to receiving it and it will act accordingly.'

"The voice was beginning to fade into the distance now. As I looked into the vastness of the Universe, I saw ships, like vehicles flying across it and attacking each other with what looked like fire or bullets. It seems that the same kind of problems that we have on Earth also exist, and continue to exist, elsewhere throughout the Universe. However, now the view surrounding me is beginning to change, and I am being drawn towards a planet."

Chapter 15

Cydonia: The Face on Mars

Cydonia Mars - Shuttlestock

"I can hear Aleaze's voice, 'Yes, this is the planet Mars', he says. Then, as we draw closer, I see a rusty red coloured looking planet, and Aleaze starts speaking again."

"Mars is an arid and dusty planet, slightly more than half the size of your Earth. It has temperatures of minus 143c degrees to 35c degrees from its polar regions to the equatorial summers. There are craters all over the planet. Mars has two moons. At one time, Mars had a similar environment to Earth, and then there was a cataclysm. The oceans washed over the planet and changed its atmosphere to a dry and dusty red environment. Nuclear explosions created debris all over Mars. It was due to an alien invasion that wiped out most of its civilization. I want you to look closely now and tell me what you see."

"As I stared, I could see craters and rocks on its surface. Aleaze told me to look closer. I continued to do so and began to see what looked like a face! It was a huge face with some headdress surrounding it. I asked him, what is this, a face on Mars, or is it another illusion, just like many others that we believe in, or not?"

"Yes." Aleaze said, "The face exists and is around two kilometres long. It is situated in Cydonia, where one of the nuclear explosions took place. If you look closely, you will see a great pyramid to the southwest of it. To the northwest of the face, there lies a city complex of twelve pyramids. There is also a huge manufactured mount."

"After Aleaze spoke, we were silent. I gazed out upon what I had seen and heard; it was all so unbelievable. Yet, there is a feeling that touches my heart, which seems so true! As I was about to ask Aleaze another question, a strange sensation rushed through me. I was not sure at that moment where I was or whether I was in my physical body. Suddenly, there was a feeling of confusion, like a whirlwind sweeping across and taking me to somewhere else, then moving towards peace and calmness. Something was happening to me, and I was beginning to experience a physical sensation, as though I were reconnecting with my body. It was all happening so fast, and then I found myself back in the small hut at the concentration camp where it all began. Throughout the journey, I had forgotten all about my life in the camp. It was as though I had never been born into this world before, and the world had never existed. I experienced feelings of being a part of a whole, a sense of oneness in the present, and that is all there was and nothing else! Now I am back here, where life is so different. Then Aleaze appeared and spoke."

"Everything is an illusion; nothing is permanent. It applies to everything, even when you gaze at the night sky and see the stars. These stars are still visible to the naked eye, yet what you are seeing is how they were thousands of years ago because of how light travels, said Aleaze."

Rosa continued...

"I am experiencing what appears to be hell in this camp. Although each time that I journey through the Cosmos, I become more detached from the mental and physical restraints of this world. I now also question things and ask myself who I am! The more I do this, my focus on the subject disappears, and everything becomes void, empty and clear, and far beyond the conscious state of my mind. It helps me immensely to cope whilst I am here, as I now have no feelings for this world anymore. Yet, somehow, I still live in the hope that one day it will all be different.

"I am back in the barracks now, with the other women, and for some reason, one of them is approaching me. What does she want? Has she seen something of my disappearance? 'Your mother is ill', she says.

"This has been my worst fear, and now it has happened. I ask what is wrong with my mother. The woman says, 'your mother collapsed when she returned to the barracks from work'. I quickly rush over to my mother and find her in a semi-conscious state, slowly drifting in and out of consciousness. I sit beside her and hold her hand in the very cramped conditions on the small wooden bunk beds that we sleep in. I could see that she had developed a fever and was suffering from exhaustion. I could only hope that the fever would break quickly. If anyone appeared weak in any way, they dealt with them immediately by removing them from the barracks and work. They would generally take them to another barracks where they left them to die, without food or water.

"I had to get in touch with Aleaze; it was my mother's only chance to recover and survive. I tried hard to communicate throughout the night by using telepathy, which I had developed with him. However, for some reason, it was not working. I was not making a connection. Perhaps it was because I was trying too hard and panicking with fear of losing my mother. As the night continued, my mother seemed to become stronger. It was amazing, the fever had broken, and she had regained consciousness. She sat up as if nothing was wrong. I could not believe it, and as I looked at her, she said, 'I feel fine Rosa, it was as if someone appeared to me, who looked like an angel and passed their hands over me. Then, there was a golden light, and as it began to fade, this person, or whoever they were, disappeared. After that, I began to recover and gained my strength, feeling stronger than before'.

"In a relieved voice, I told her how worried I had been for her. 'I am OK', she replied. Deep down, my mother was a strong woman who did not always express her true feelings. After both of her parents were killed during the last war, she had to survive by herself. Perhaps she learned to suppress her feelings during this lonely time.

"The next day, it was back to work, rising for roll call at 4 am. Due to my mother's quick recovery, she was able to continue with the work. Later on that day, I was able to meet Aleaze and return to the small hut. As soon as I saw him, I greeted him with great joy and thanked him for my mother's speedy recovery. He answered me and said, 'but it was not me.' I was confused and told him that my mother had told me that she saw someone come to her and then a light appeared and disappeared, and after this, she felt fine. 'No, it was not me, I'm sorry, but I really could not help this time. Everything had to take its natural course', said Aleaze. I asked him how this could have been. 'Actually, I do not know. It seems that an angel who healed her visited your mother. Of course, this was her faith that made it happen,' said Aleaze.

"So there are angels, I said. 'Yes, there are many beings of all descriptions. Some angels help in many different ways, and this was one of them, watching over your mother'.

"Aleaze continued to speak, 'I am going to take you on another journey now, one that may be a final destination, or so it might seem.' I wondered what Aleaze had meant but didn't question him."

Chapter 16

Beyond Past Lives and the Anunnaki

"Aleaze called out to me...are you ready? I was becoming a little more familiar with his appearance now than during my first experience in this small hut.

"Yes, I answered him, staring ahead. Everything was starting to become void, and one with the vastness of the Universe. I could see beautiful and unique outbursts and explosions of colour, creating strobes of light that spread out across the Milky Way. I recall that someone or something told me that there was a gateway connecting with the Universe, it is where all things can be seen, and the knowledge is shared. I could feel that my body was turning into particles, melding into the great Universe and its oneness.

"Somewhere in the distance, there was what looked like a planet. It could be Earth, although I am not sure. As we were drawn towards it, I noticed the colours green and blue. Suddenly, it seemed that I was moving towards this planet at a very high speed and about to crash into it with great force. I had no idea what was happening. I felt dizzy and had difficulty focussing. I had become perplexed, and everything was spinning. I must have passed out, as I do not remember what happened, although my eyes were open, and I could feel that my body was intact.

"I was on a planet, and for some reason, I felt that it might be Earth. Yet, everything looked very different; there were no buildings, only trees and forestry, which looked like mountains in the distance. Then, suddenly, Aleaze appeared again beside me. Shaking a little, I asked him what had happened to me, and he replied."

"Yes, that was quite a journey, and you are on Earth. We are now in a different time zone; you have entered the past, way back in time. The Earth has replenished several times, and it will continue to do so in the future. It is a way of cleansing.

"There have always been opposing forces since the creation of this world. The evil or the negative energy works with the good, the positive energy; its purpose is to help humans evolve. Unfortunately, the human race must suffer. Although much of the suffering is due to ignorance, the evil forces bring one closer to self-realization, to the higher self, and thus to know oneself. When you begin to understand your true selves, everything starts to change around us, even the world. When all humans realise that there is no separation and you are all one, there will be true peace; until that time, it will be as it is.

"One reason why Earth replenishes itself is that its population has not learned lessons. Even though they have been shown ways to live, and have been given guidance by advanced intelligent beings from other galaxies, still the advice has been ignored. For example, one of the earliest races to come to Earth was called, The Ancient Ones. They were very advanced in many ways. After that period in time came the Anunnaki, which was around 450,000 years ago. This race created conflict, and wars began with the Ancient Ones.

"The Ancient ones fought large scale battles with the Anunnaki and then returned to their home world. The Anunnaki remained on Earth using humans as slaves to do their work.

"The Anunnaki went on to become the gods of Heaven and Earth. They had superior knowledge and power. They also laid claim to the creation of man. It is shown on clay tablets, containing one of the earliest forms of writing known as Cuneiform. This form of writing; was developed by the Sumerians of Mesopotamia, now modern-day Iraq.

"The Anunnaki also fought wars amongst themselves. The Babylonian God Ea, who was victorious in battle, was made their leader. He was the son of Anu and husband of Damkina Earth goddess, and father of Marduk. When the sons of Anu arrived at the Valley of the Two Rivers, they brought with them three tablets. These tablets were shiny like bronze and carried a wealth of power and knowledge. During these conflicts and the many wars and battles that occurred, the tablets of destinies were lost. Without these tablets, there was little hope of gaining victory.

"The God Kingu was given the tablets by his wife, who was the original owner. Kingu took them and sealed them on his breast in the hope of defeating the other gods. However, this never happened, as Marduk overpowered him. He then took the tablets, placed them around his neck, and became King of the Universe. The three tablets of destinies held the secrets to the Earth, the oceans and the Universe; they also represented past, present and future. These tablets contained the knowledge of how to live for centuries on Earth and travel far at high speeds. All could be seen through the tablets, which gave great power to whoever possessed them. In ancient Egypt, in the book of Thoth, there was mention of two tablets containing great magic, knowledge and secrets of the Universe. Unfortunately, the tablets were stolen," Aleaze said.

Chapter 17

Cloning

DNA - The Tree of Life - Shuttlestock

"Aleaze continued speaking to me."

"The Anunnaki saw that there were gold and other minerals on earth. They decided to mine them, creating a small colony on the planet. They did this in the knowledge that it would be easier not to have to do the physical work themselves. Marduk, their leader, took blood from Kingu, the God who was sacrificed and slain. Marduk then mixed Kingu's blood with clay to create a human on earth. The Bible tells a similar story of Adam, who was made from clay.

"The Anunnaki did what humans are now beginning to do in modern times; they changed the DNA or deoxyribonucleic acid. This is the hereditary material in humans and other living things. They created new species of animals and humans, cloning them to produce exact replicas, genetically identical. They took the DNA from one species and impregnated another species with it. Humans are not the same as other animals; they have one different gene.

"The original forms of life on earth may have been created from clay. The process that eventually formed protein, DNA and living cells could have taken billions of years. In Genesis, in the Bible, it says; that God created Adam from a handful of soil, which contained all the varieties of the earth. Angels were then sent down to earth to collect some of your soil, then God gave the breath-of-life from his nostrils, and a living being was created!

"All things are possible in many ways and many forms. The extra-terrestrials did not claim themselves as gods at first. Their purpose was to use humans for work. Over time, other beings were created through genetic experiments, such as the dinosaurs. They also created half animals and half-humans, for instance, the Centaur, half-human and half horse, and the Cyclops, a giant with one eye and some dragons that breathed fire. Other extra-terrestrials came to earth and experimented with creating strange creatures. You may have read about them in fairy-tale books for children. These creatures were wiped out every time a replenishment occurred.

"There is the belief that humans evolved from apes, and some will continue to search for the missing link between them. However, they will not find this because they are separate species, even though they are both related. If there was an evolvement between the two, then why do apes still exist? It will be a choice for most to believe in either a creator or everything is created accidentally. Yet, in reality, there are no accidents, as everything has its purpose!

"After the DNA was manipulated creating reasonably intelligent human beings, the humans or Homo Sapiens continued to work for the Anunnaki as slaves. As time passed, they showed humans some arts and skills and a guide on how to live as humans; they also introduced the science of astrology and many other things.

"Something similar is written in the Torah and Bible, telling the story of fallen Angels who became the Watchers. The Watchers were to watch over humanity and report back, about their progress. These may have been the Anunnaki, who came down to earth and took women for themselves. The women bore children, who produced mutant offspring. In Genesis 6:1, the oldest book in the Hebrew Bible, it says...

'...And it came to pass when men began to multiply on the face of the earth, and daughters were born to them, that the sons of God saw the daughters of men, that they were beautiful and took them wives of all which they chose'.

There were many who were called the Sons of God, who were in their appearance; like humans. Two hundred in all, with their leader Semjaza, descended to earth on the summit of Mount Hermon, between Lebanon and the Golan Heights. Genesis continues, '...There were giants in the earth in those days. And after that, when the sons of God came in unto the daughters of men, and they bore children to them, the same became mighty men which were of old, men of renown.'

"One of the leaders, Azazel, taught humans how to make swords, breastplates, knives and shields. Semjaza taught enchantments and root cuttings; others showed women how to adorn themselves by making mirrors, jewellery, dyes, and paints to make cosmetics. Humans were introduced to precious stones and medicine making and taught the signs of the Clouds, Earth, Sun, Moon, and the constellations.

"The children produced by the Anunnaki, or the Fallen Angels and the Daughters of Earth, were called the Nephilim. The Nephilim were the giants on earth that tormented the humans. When humans could no longer support the Nephilim and had no meat to give them, the

Nephilim turned against the humans and began to devour them.

"After this time, the four angels Michael, Uriel, Raphael, and Gabriel; looked down from heaven, saw the bloodshed and the lawlessness and reported it to the higher power. It was seen that what had been created was not good. Then a replenishment began with the Deluge, flooding and washing the earth and its population, as is shown in the Sumerian texts.

"The same thing happened before, which led to a cataclysmic disaster with the legendary lost continent of Lemuria, Atlantis, and perhaps others that have been lost. During these previous times of the Anunnaki, the humans began to rebel against slavery and demanded their freedom. Eventually, it was given to them, and the Anunnaki finally left and went back home.

"The Anunnaki had occupied bases all over the world. These beings were tall like giants; many had blonde hair and blue eyes. They had a symbol, which was a winged disc. This symbol is shown on the walls and writings of ancient Babylonia and Sumeria. The symbol shows an

Anunnaki or king in the air with a disc, which is his Starship. Hitler; ordered much research on extra-terrestrials and other phenomena to use these magical powers to create an Aryan race of tall, blonde and blue-eyed humans, also known as the Nordics. These Nordics would eventually take over and conquer the world."

Chapter 18

Return to Ravensbrück and the Ark

Ark of the Covenant - Shuttlestock

Rosa started to talk again.

"Aleaze finally halted in his words. As he spoke about all of this, the creation of the world, and other unimaginable things, I began to see Ravensbrück, the Concentration Camp. Yet this time, I was not there in my physical body, only as an observer. I could see that many women were being moved out of the camp. There must have been a thousand or more. They appeared to be mainly German Jewish women, although they may have been Gypsies of Romany origin. It looked as though they were moving towards Poland.

"Oh my God, it is a new camp called Auschwitz Birkenau for women; I have heard such horror stories of Auschwitz. Now I can see my mother, and she is walking with the others from the barracks. I am calling out to her…Mother, Mother. Aleaze tells me that she cannot see me or hear me. Frantically I say to him that I must get to her, or what will become of her? He tells me not to worry and that she will be OK. However, I knew that this was a death camp. It is a terrible place where they kill everyone. Again, Aleaze promises me that she will be OK, and I have to take his word for it, as I am helpless here.

"Aleaze carried on talking, and I found it difficult to concentrate. I listened to what he had to say, which went something like this."

"Throughout the whole time on Earth, humans have witnessed and have had encounters with other beings from different galaxies. They have experienced the phenomena of seeing those who have descended from the heavens above.

"The prophet Ezekiel spoke of a whirlwind about a fire that came from the North. In its midst were the likenesses of four living creatures that resembled humans. Each one had four faces and four wings. Beneath their wings were the forms of human hands. A human face was on the front, and on the right side was the face of a lion. An Ox could be seen on the left side, and an eagle was visible on the back. Some wheels were lifted over them; the spirit of the living creatures was in the wheels.

"A whirlwind also took the prophet, Elijah, to heaven, as well as others in ancient history. Moses, too, encountered a tremendous force on Mount Sinai when speaking with his creator. After spending forty days on the mountain under a thick cloud and darkness, Moses was given two stone tablets of the laws. When Moses descended from Mount Sinai, he was unaware how his face shone, glowing radiantly, and this frightened his people. After that time, Moses always covered his face.

"God told Moses to tell his followers; that he would come down to all of the people on Mount Sinai. He also told them not to climb the mountain or touch the edge, as whoever did so would be put to death. Mount Sinai was covered in smoke as God descended on it in the form of fire. The smoke then ascended and billowed up into the sky like a great furnace, and the whole mountain shook violently. When the people saw the thunder and lightning and heard the sound of the trumpet, they trembled with fear and kept their distance.

"When Moses was last on the mountain, his God had instructed him to have a Tabernacle and an Ark built; this should not be confused with the Ark of Noah and the floods. Chief artisan, Bezalel, constructed the Ark one year after the Israelites exodus from Egypt. On his descent from the mountain, Moses placed the tablets of the law in the Ark.

"After Moses had been away on Mount Sinai, he realised that his people had begun to worship an idol of a golden calf. They needed a place to worship. Although it had been commanded to be built sometime earlier, this was the purpose of The Tabernacle. The Ark of the Covenant was carried in the desert by the Israelites for forty years. The Tabernacle (a tent) was a sanctuary for worship and a resting place for the Ark of the Covenant.

"The reason I am bringing this to your attention, Rosa, is that it was the tribe of Levi that was in charge of erecting and dismantling the Tabernacle. They were also in charge of carrying the Ark as well. Only they were allowed to handle it. Your bloodline traces back to the tribe of Levi. You are a direct descendant of them."

"As Aleaze spoke of this, everything resonated within my soul, like a mild electrifying current running through me. Was it just a feeling? No, I knew somehow that I was, or had been, part of this event that had taken place in the desert, with the Israelites, so long ago. I could see that Aleaze had a lot more to tell me about the Ark as he continued his tale."

"The Ark was a chest made of Acacia wood and overlaid with gold inside and out; it was around four feet long, two and a half feet wide and two and a half feet in height. It was fitted with rings of gold at each corner to pass through poles for carrying it. On top of the chest, there was a pure gold covering called a Kapporet. Attached to the Kapporet, two golden cherubs faced each other with their wings spread open. When Moses entered the Tabernacle, he would hear the voice of God speak between the two Cherubs, and a glowing cloud was visible. The Ark had certain powers. One was levitation. It rose and hovered in the air, carrying its bearer inches above the ground. It could also clear the paths of snakes, scorpions and thorns, with two jets of flame that shot out from underneath.

"The Ark was carried by the Israelites, leading them into battle. The first battle took place in Jericho. The men of war were around three thousand. They were told to circle the city once a day for six days with the Ark and seven priests. They marched around the city walls seven times; the seven priests blew their Rams Horns. When they heard the sounds of the horns, the people shouted out. After this, the walls of the city collapsed. Under the Herem, the Jewish law, they spared no one who dwelt in the City of Jericho. All the men, women, children and animals living there were slaughtered with the edge of the sword. The only person spared was a prostitute named Rahab and her family; they had sheltered the messenger of Joshua, who had been sent to spy in the city.

"The powers of the Ark were seen to be dangerous when worshipping it inside the Tabernacle. Aaron, Moses older brother, had two sons Nadab and Abihu, who came to visit, offering a sacrifice. As the sons approached the Ark, they held containers with fire inside and incense burning. The Ark reacted, perceiving that they might be posing a threat to it. As a result, both the sons were devoured by fire. After that time, the Ark remained in the Tabernacle for almost four hundred years.

"Eventually, the Israelites took the Ark into battle. During the second battle, which they lost to their opponents the Ark was captured; then the Philistines took it away. The Philistines kept it for seven months then returned it to the Israelites. Wherever the Philistines took the Ark, misfortune fell upon them with plagues in every city, and whoever gazed at it was smitten.

"Under instruction from King David, the driver of a cart was moving the Ark; as he touched the Ark to steady it, he was struck dead. After that, the Ark was always covered in silk, and a blue cloth lay over it. Eventually, it was brought to Jerusalem. After this time, the Ark and its location were never mentioned again. Some believe it may have been destroyed with the temple of Jerusalem when King Nebuchadnezzar of Babylon burned down the city or that he may have taken it with him. Others say that he hid it beneath the temple mount, an Islamic holy site called the Dome of the Rock. There is one theory that Jeremiah took it up Mount Nebo. He found a room in a cave, placed the tent and the Ark inside and sealed the entrance.

"Another theory is that the Queen of Sheba visited King Solomon from South Arabia, modern-day Yemen. He warmly welcomed her at his temple in Jerusalem. During her short stay with Solomon, the Queen of Sheba became pregnant, and on her return, she gave birth to a son called Menelik. His original name was BäynäLəhkəm, meaning Son of the Wise. When Menelik grew up, he travelled to Jerusalem with others from Ethiopia. After seeing his father, it is said that he secretly took the

Ark with him. However, rumour has it that the Ark spent three or four hundred years in Egypt before it arrived in Ethiopia. The Ethiopian Orthodox Church now claims to have the Ark of the Covenant in Axim, Ethiopia.

"Therefore, Rosa, as you can see, there is much mysticism in the heavens and on Earth. Many things are hidden, which are yet to be found. They will be revealed when the time comes. Until now, human beings have not been ready to receive knowledge that will enhance their mental capacity towards enlightenment.

"Even though you are all still relatively primitive, things are changing fast in this world and the Universe. These changes give you many opportunities for greater awareness and understanding that you are all from one source. There is no separation. Many children will be born into this world to change the course of humanity and help others understand how to create harmony and unconditional love throughout the planet. There will always be those who resist changes, and there will always be those who strive for control. The children of the light will go to war with the children of the dark, a war that will last for six years. Although, eventually, all will realise after almost destroying the planet and themselves that enough is enough and the suffering of humankind must end. Even though this will happen, there will be an intervention from the heavens before peace on Earth is accomplished."

Chapter 19

Alien Technology

Black Sun - Wikipedia

Rosa continued.

"As I took time to contemplate all that Aleaze had described, I saw somewhere that reminded me of Germany. Although this time, it was not the camp I knew or any camp for that matter. I could see a castle, and inside was a basement or crypt. There was a room, in the crypt where twelve men stood around in a circle. In the centre of the room was a small pit with an eternal flame, lit by gas, as far as I could tell. I knew some of these men, as I had seen their photos in newspapers. One of them was Heinrich Himmler; he was the leader of the Nazi party. Aleaze once more began to speak."

"Yes, this man is also responsible for the Holocaust, and under Hitler's orders, he set up the Nazi concentration and extermination camps. The castle you see belongs to Himmler and is called Wewelsburg."

Rosa carried on with her tale, but her voice trembled as she responded to the vision before her eyes.

"I see another man; he looks like Hermann Goering, the head of the Gestapo. There are others, generals of the SS. I can see another room above, a hall, in the shape of a circle. White columns support arches, rectangular windows are between each column. In the centre of the room, set into the marble floor, is a mosaic pattern of some kind."

"Yes," said Aleaze, "it was an occult symbol, a Black Sun. They used these rooms for satanic rituals and tried to contact beings from other worlds. For example, the Nazis set up a secret society called Vril. They took the name from a book written many years before called, The Coming Race, by Edward Bulwer-Lytton. They also used beautiful, psychic girls to help contact beings and spirits.

"Himmler's ideology was to create the centre of a new world. The room they used for this purpose was called the Centre of the World. In 1936, on the edge of the Black Forest, near Freiburg in Germany, a silver shaped disc crashed to Earth. Soon it was reported, and immediately, the Nazis investigated. Inside the craft, they found beings from another world. Shortly after that, they removed the vessel and the beings to Wewelsburg Castle. From this time onwards, Germany became advanced in technology. It was the first nation to discover nuclear energy, which will lead to the development of the atomic bomb.

"After the war ended, Von Braun, the Scientist who invented the V1 and V2 rockets, was taken to work in the USA to develop the moon rockets. When the spacecraft crashed on the edge of the Black Forest, Von Braun was one of the first to arrive at the scene. He said, upon arrival, that the crafts material felt as though it was made from some form of skin.

"Another crash happened in 1947, somewhere near Roswell, New Mexico, in the United States of America, where they found bodies of other beings from another world. Von Braun was present at that scene too. Again, he said the craft was of a strange metal, thin and almost like skin.

"The beings inside the craft were said to be of a reptilian species. Before that time, when Von Braun and another scientist, Hermann Ober, were under investigation, they were asked about how they made their advancement in technology. They both answered that people from other worlds helped them.

"More than sixteen hundred scientists, engineers and technicians were taken to the USA, under a secret operation, called Paperclip. Top Nazi doctors and others, of great importance to the American government, accompanied them. In August of 1945, Operation Paperclip culminated in the United States dropping an atomic bomb on Japan, killing 129,000 people and ending the war! Dr Wernher Von Braun eventually became the Director of NASA, founded in 1958 in the USA. NASA stands for National Aeronautical and Space Administration."

"After Aleaze told me this, with the war ending, I became confused about what was the present and what was the future. I was also curious to know what had happened to my family. Aleaze answered immediately."

"They are safe, and you will know everything very soon."

"Strangely enough, I said nothing and felt calm as I waited for him to continue with what he had to say."

"You see, Rosa, through the secret organisation known as Vril, they searched for the Ark of the Covenant, the Holy Grail and other holy relics. The Nazis took and used many things from the past. For example, the Swastika was an ancient symbol dating 12,000 years ago. It is a Sanskrit name meaning Good Fortune, used in Hinduism, Buddhism, Jainism, and other cultures worldwide. The Nazis used this symbol for power. It also led them to the rediscovery of Vimanas, the flying machines of ancient India, the chariots of the gods."

"When Aleaze had finished speaking to me, I replied, although some of the things he was saying had slipped my mind because I was thinking of my family. Nonetheless, it was very intriguing. Now I can see why the Nazis were interested in creating an Aryan race. They wanted to become super-human, destroying anything and anyone that did not meet their requirements. They became obsessed with researching anything related to space and time and antiquities going back to ancient biblical times. They were also interested in the Occult, in using it to manipulate and gain power. Luckily, most things are lost that may have once held magical powers."

Chapter 20

The Gateway

"After Aleaze and I had finished communicating with each other, I began to drift away once again, into the vast Universe. I can see a gateway connecting with the Universe, where all things can be seen and knowledge shared. My body, if I had one at that moment in time, felt as though it was becoming particles, dissolving into the great Universe and Oneness.

"I saw a gateway that seemed to connect with Earth and other planets, and I saw the ancient monuments of the world all aligned to planets like Orion and Nibiru. Furthermore, I could see that these ancient monuments were pointing towards the star constellation of Leo and Orion and two other significant planets, known as Pleiades and Sirius Minor. Beings came from these planets to visit Earth, and humans perceived them as gods. Many were messengers, and some came to teach.

"I now know that there were those who harmed humans. Like the Nephilim, the giants, the descendants of the fallen angels. These star beings were superhuman and had great powers, although some of their abilities came from their tools. Many Nephilim, who helped the humans, used these tools to build the ancient monuments. They used tools to cut and carve out the stone with total precision, to the point that even a hair of the head would be unable to pass between the rocks as they sat tightly against each other.

"In these modern times, we struggle to find the answers to how these ancient sites, throughout the world were built. Even one of the great pyramids in Egypt, which was exactly twice the size of the ones in Central America, shows a connection. There have been tales of strange crafts and beings that descended to Earth, in myths and stories worldwide.

"Some of these beings were in Atlantis, then in ancient Egypt, Mexico and Central and South America. This ancient history also dates back to the Sumerians, Babylonia, and the Anunnaki, who had all the knowledge.

"I can see the power of three encoded in what is now called DNA. This discovery leads back to the beginning of humanity, as the discovery of the stone tablets of this time does. These discoveries may have had some significance to the Ark and its powers. They depict the god Marduk taking the blood from the god Kingu and mixing it with clay to create a human.

"The Anunnaki were physical beings that came from other worlds. They changed the DNA initially found in the previous more primitive humans to create more intelligent humans. One of the Anunnaki Kings was said to have lived for 35,000 years; since that time, the ages declined; Moses lived to 900 years, Noah to 950. Eventually, after the floods, man was given the average time to live to around seventy years.

"The Anunnaki were originally from the Planet Nibiru and came to Earth around 450,000 years ago. These beings had elongated cone-shaped heads, and the Nephilim were their offspring. Queen Puabi, a descendant of the Anunnaki who lived in Mesopotamia, modern-day Iraq, also had an elongated skull, similar to some Peruvians living in South America (and in Ancient Egypt). In addition, the Anunnaki wore a wristband, looking like a watch, or perhaps something else that may have been important to them. Were these our ancestors, the Anunnaki, who may have created us through genetic manipulation?"

"Yes," said Aleaze, "now you understand what has happened in the Cosmos and on Earth. They came and said, 'Let us make man in our own image,' although the Anunnaki were not the total creators. They changed the DNA and body of the primitive ancestors, creating a more intelligent being. However, they did not create the original source's energy, which is the Soul."

"I wanted to ask Aleaze, 'then who did?' Something stopped me. Perhaps I did not want to know, and somehow, I felt relief that there was so much more to comprehend about the creation of the Universe! It was only the beginning of knowing who we were and understanding our Higher Self. It works for the good of others and knows that we were not created only to be slaves and then die.

"Yet, I believe that there is another side to it all. There is an opposite with everything that exists: unconditional love, creating balance, which is how the Universe was created."

"Indeed," said Aleaze, "Everything in the Universe resonates at a high frequency. Therefore, those who have descended to Earth are the ones who have created change in humanity. It is inevitable, as whatever happens will happen."

"I decided to ask Aleaze another question; 'who created the Anunnaki?' He replied..."

"I can only say that those who were responsible for the changes on Earth were two men who came to this planet from Nibiru. Their names were Enlil and Enki. Anu was their father, the King of Nibiru. As I said before, they taught the humans many skills in exchange for their labour, mining for gold and other minerals. However, humans learned these skills after Enlil and Enki used them as slaves.

Anunnaki - Wikipedia

"The Anunnaki gave the ancient Egyptians a symbol, called the Ankh; this symbol represented Heaven and Earth. The Anunnaki also assisted in building many ancient monuments around the world. The pyramids of Giza in Egypt were amongst them. The largest pyramid was the King's pyramid, made of two and a half million stone blocks. Although the workers built the pyramids, the Anunnaki had the knowledge and expertise to guide them. A certain kind of geometry was used in the building called 'Tetrahedral'. It was the same geometry used for the pyramids on Mars, with a highly sophisticated form of mathematics.

"Most of the ancient monuments built on Earth align with the star systems of Orion, Leo and Draco. The great pyramid lines up with Orion in the King's chamber, and the Queen's chamber aligns with Sirius. The ancient Egyptians believed that Isis, the wife of Osiris, who used magic spells to help people in need, was from Sirius, and Osiris was from Orion.

"The Dogon tribe of Mali in West Africa is believed to be descended from ancient Egyptians. The Nommos, from the Sirius star system, visited these Dogons thousands of years ago. The Nommos were amphibious reptilians, the same who visited Sumer. The Dogons say that the visitor's upper body was like a man, with the lower body like a snake; this has also been seen in ancient Hindu mythology. The Dogons called them 'The Masters of the Water'. They came to teach them and show them where they were from, long before the rest of the world discovered the star system of Sirius.

"On this Earth, a lot of things connected to the Universe have appeared as strange to humans. After the great flood of Noah, recorded in the Sumerian texts, the memory of the Anunnaki was lost, amongst many other things. Although, there were always remnants to be found, scattered around the world. Archaeologists will continue to find objects and sites. Eventually, much of the truth will be revealed and no longer repressed.

"As well as monuments and structures built in ancient times, there is evidence of skeletons and giants buried worldwide. In Ancient Egypt, elongated skulls of some Pharaohs and Queens were found, just as they were discovered in the caves of Peru. These and the Sumerians were the descendants of the Anunnaki or the hybrids of this alien race.

"The pyramids of Egypt and many other sites can be seen from high above, just like the Nazca lines in South America, which are only possible to see from the air. Mandalas can be seen from the top of high temple construction in Indonesia. These are significant as they shine like beacons; that may be seen from above, perhaps to show where to land.

"That is why these man-made structures all align with each other to the planets. On Earth, even below the depths of the oceans, there are bases for alien crafts because there have been reports of strange flying machines rising from the ocean. There have also been many sightings by locals from Lake Titicaca in Bolivia, the highest navigable lake in the world, of flying objects surfacing from the lake. Local people have seen these objects for many years. Native American Indians have also made close contact with visitors from other worlds!"

Chapter 21

A Creation of Angels and Beings of Pure Consciousness

Angel - a collection by G Markwick

"I thanked Aleaze for sharing his knowledge with me and decided to ask some more questions; I was too hesitant to do so before. I asked him if the Anunnaki were not our original creators, then who or what was. This is what Aleaze said."

"Again, I cannot answer directly. I can only say that the creators were not of this world and that the one who rules now will not do so forever. When this time comes, there will be peace on Earth."

"I also asked Aleaze about the Angels to tell me who or what they are."

"The Greek word Aggelos and the Hebrew word Mal'ak has the same meaning...Messenger. They are messengers. Many believe Angels are purely spiritual beings. This is true, but they also have the power to transform into humans and live on Earth in a physical body. Angels were not created in the same way as men or women. Angels are angelic beings. As in everything, there is good and evil within them too. Remember, the Fallen Angels came to Earth, took the daughters of men for their wives, and then fathered the unnatural offspring of the Nephilim. It has been said that a thousand Angels were created; as they do not die, they will remain this way forever. Throughout time, Angels have appeared to humans. They have often been seen as beings in radiant, dazzling light.

So, Rosa, you have now seen, heard and witnessed many things."

"I replied that if Angels have these powers, then why are they not stopping all the terrible things happening in this world, and why has God not intervened? Aleaze answered."

"There have always been battles, in the Heavens and on Earth. However, greater power and plans guide the destinies of all nations, when eventually good will rise above evil. I can only say to you, Rosa, that you are all beings of pure consciousness, more than just your bodies. When you are in the self, you move beyond the external world, and true happiness exists when you remain within the real self."

"How is this possible, I questioned Aleaze, when we have been tortured and starved and have had to watch our loved ones perish before our very eyes?"

"There has been a force of evil which created suffering since the beginning of the Earths creation. However, as I have said before, good and evil work together to bring humans closer to the self, the oneness of the higher power. Eventually, people will cry out to end the suffering of humankind! It will not be easy for you to detach from the physical senses of the Lower Self and realise the Higher Self. This is especially so when your body and mind meet with the attachments and atrocities of the material World. However, when you can do this and reach self-realisation, you will come to know your true self and have the ability to remove yourself from the Worlds suffering. Then you will know that there is no death, only an eternal soul. This soul continues on its journey until it reaches its final destination after so many incarnations. Death is the sleeping state after leaving one life on Earth before entering the next re-birth. Those who have departed before you in the present lifetime were freed from bondage. Therefore, there is no need to grieve for them for so long; much of the grieving is often for yourselves. The ego needs to be destroyed before you can be freed from the fear of death!"

"I answered him, even though I was a little angered and at the same time feeling that I should now be freed from anything that was creating restrictions on my soul. I told him that when you have been so close to the ones you love; and they die suddenly, knowing that you will never see them again has a traumatic effect. On Earth, we show love to those who are close to us and we show empathy or sympathy to those who may not be so close. Aleaze answered."

"Love is the greatest thing, but often the love shared amongst you is possessive. Unconditional love is letting go when the time comes and surrendering without the need for control. It is not necessarily the case that you will not see loved ones again. There may be many reasons for you to connect with them in another life. It might be in another form, depending on what you need to learn. Conditional love creates possessiveness, anger, hate, blame, violence and guilt. When there is unconditional love, it produces greatness of self and others, which is selfless. The greatest way to help others, besides forgiveness, is to create self-awareness, with good intentions that it may be recognised. Let go externally, but still keep within the pure essence in peace, happiness and oneness, as there is no separation!"

"I cannot deny what Aleaze said, but it is hard not to be affected by what happens in our lives. So, I told Aleaze he was right and that it was natural for humans to experience these emotions. Aleaze responded."

"Yes, I understand. Therefore, you must grieve and move on when you can. However, it will become easier when you experience a greater awareness of the Higher Self. There is no need for control when you remain in the self, as nothing else exists."

Chapter 22

Earth School

"I asked Aleaze how I may attain this self-realization, he answered."

"Actually, you are already there, as you are always The Self. Everything else that exists is external to the body. So, you are more than the body!"

"What Aleaze said helped me to see things with more clarity. I sense that I am beginning to understand now that everything of the Higher Self is contained within us. Everything takes care of itself when we concentrate on this State-of-Being. We should worry no longer because what will be will be. We must accept this and allow the changes, whatever they may be. Although, I believe the most challenging thing to do is go beyond the fear and face the unknown.

"I have learnt so much from Aleaze on this journey in time that crossed the Earth and the Universe. I know now that when we experience horrors, atrocities, and the loss of those we love, this will eventually bring us closer to our souls and the higher power of the source. The Earth is a learning school - Earth School! We repeat the same mistakes until we learn not to do so. Then, when we are ready to move on to the next phase or level, we do, wherever or whatever that may be.

"We move from being a child to an adult, from one who is uneducated to becoming an intellectual, then from intellectualism to intellectual awareness. From there, we go from intellectual awareness to higher awareness and then on to enlightenment. There is no need for struggle and strife when one has found The Self. Somehow, it all seems like a game and perhaps that is the whole plan? Aleaze started to speak again."

"Now you are on the journey of your Higher Self."

"I questioned this in my thoughts for a moment and then accepted it. As I did this once again, I began to see my mother; she was boarding a train to another camp with others. I can also see that the war is finally over, and I can see that the Americans liberated my mother.

"After a while, I saw my father, whom I thought had perished. He had been taken to other camps and somehow he had survived. Eventually, my parents found each other. After travelling to London, England, they were reunited with their son, my brother Benjamin.

"I wondered where I was and why I had not returned to the camp with my mother and then transferred to another campsite with everyone else. Even though I had not spoken, Aleaze answered, he said."

"You had not realised, but you also contracted a fever, and because the food was scarce and work was difficult, you did not make it any further in that life."

"I should have known this, so I asked him what is real, and he replied."

"That which is of the external world is an illusion your true path within is eternal. Even though everything is an illusion externally, all you experienced exists beyond Earth School."

"As Aleaze spoke to me, I felt that something was changing. The energy was shifting. I was now moving towards a doorway or a gateway in the Universe. Ahead of me was a haze so bright that I could not see anything else.

I drifted into it and experienced peace and tranquillity. So peaceful that nothing else existed, only unconditional love and a feeling that was so powerful that I cannot describe it to you. Then Aleaze continued with his explanation."

"You are now in the Interlife, a place between lives. The Interlife is where you may let go and forgive anything or anyone from the life that you have just left. So, what have you learnt from your previous life? Is there anyone whom you may need to forgive?"

"Aleaze asked me this question, calling me by my name. I answered that I could say I hated those responsible for the mass murders in the camps and those who tortured their victims and made them suffer so much that they wanted to die; so that they might be free. I could also say how I might have hatred inside me and that I can never let go and forgive, but no, I have learned and have gone beyond the Lower Self. If I could not do this, I would be holding so much resentment, anger and hatred within me, just like those who did those terrible things on Earth.

"If my Soul was so integrated with hate, if, and when, I returned to another life, I might be the one who carries out the atrocities, who knows. The only way to progress on Earth is to forgive and send out unconditional love. It is the only way forward, hoping that one day, finally, everyone will realise this. Admittedly, it is a hard, difficult lesson that will continue until we learn from it. As I pondered these thoughts, Aleaze spoke again."

"Yes, it is the only way, and it is a hard and long journey for you all to take. Goodbye…I have enjoyed sharing the journey of Earth School with you."

"I called out to him…wait, what happens now? There must be more. There was no answer. I called to him again…Aleaze, Aleaze, but he was gone, and I wondered where I was and what I was doing here?

"Suddenly, I could see Angels around me, and it was as though I was being sucked into a vacuum at high speed. It was like a tunnel. I whirled around as I lost my senses, then everything changed. I was unsure who or what I was or where I was now. Then everything was still for the moment. I felt resistance; there was a struggle. I could sense that I was being pulled out of somewhere where I was warm and comfortable. I wondered about the people who were staring at me. Even though I cannot see them clearly, I know they are pleased to see me. Yes, now I understand. It is a new life, and I am reborn!"

Earth School

Conclusion

In writing this book, my intention is to create greater awareness and share the possibility that all things may exist, even those that are beyond our comprehension.

Being open, and having some acceptance of what we may not always understand, can free us from limiting beliefs. If we do not open ourselves to this possibility, we may be held back in our development. This will keep us stuck in the past. Being open and accepting will enable us to understand each other and the planet we inhabit. Only then, may we progress with unity and come to know our true selves, who or what we are. When we begin to understand ourselves, we will know others.

Earth School describes ancient history. It looks at where we may have originated from and what our journey may have been like over time. As nothing new exists, we are only repeating what has already happened. We are replenishing, renewing and continuing the journey from a past that we have forgotten!

Through Orla's past lives in 'Earth School', I have attempted to create an awareness of things that have happened throughout history, which may have been overlooked or hidden. I wrote this book so that we may also know who we are and not forget certain things that have happened in the past.

It is believed in our Universe alone that there are seven hundred million trillion planets. There are an infinite number of Universes. Ancient civilizations worldwide have spoken of visitations by others from different star constellations throughout history. I believe in the possibility that other species could exist on other planets and that Earth has been visited by Extra-Terrestrial beings. Equally, I think that these intelligent beings have visited different parts of the Earth hundreds of thousands of years ago, many times. Some of these visitors manipulated humans and enslaved them, to do their work. However, other extra-terrestrial beings helped us. It is also my belief that these beings will return to Earth someday. That is if they are not already here!

I intend to create awareness on all levels and share the knowledge with others who may also acknowledge a past.

This past may have been denied them and suppressed through time by dogma. Whatever happened in the past, whether it has been a hindrance or helpful to human beings, has shaped who we are in the present. We are all the result of our past, which will shape our future progression. If we are open to possibilities within our lives, this does not mean that we must become attached to them. However, by reaching a greater level of awareness, we can strengthen and change our mind-set. Focusing on what is truly important and understanding who we are, we thus create a positive outcome!

Regarding Past Life Regression, more often than not, most people who want to experience it will do so out of curiosity. Perhaps there will also be some anticipation and a little excitement to see what, if anything appears before them whilst in a trance state. However, after searching for years and not finding solutions or answers to issues and problems, some people may turn to Past Life Regression after not finding solutions in their current life.

Is it so important that one should participate in a session? Perhaps it is not; perhaps, it is a personal choice.

Although often, there is a pattern with many of those I have regressed. A similarity happens within each past life and continues to present itself in this lifetime. This may appear as a problem that the person has in their current life. The issue is discovered through a past that has been forgotten then brought forward into the person's present conscious mind. It is the memory of this past that we cannot let go of and free ourselves. However, when we recognize it for what it is, we can let go and be free of that past, rather than repeating the same pattern throughout our lives!

The question is, could we possibly have experienced and lived previous lives? In my opinion, the answer is yes. There has been so much evidence worldwide of reincarnation, especially with innocent children between the ages of three to six years old who have no preconceived ideas. Yet, these children have spoken of other lives they are familiar with and know well. We may know that nothing is permanent, and all things must pass. However, many cycles within this present life happen before we pass on from this world, whether we are aware of them or not. The Earth and the Universe also have many cycles, constantly replenishing without ending.

In conclusion, the so-called word used to describe 'death' is misinterpreted. I see it as only a temporary state of sleep between two lives, of which there are many! We may start to learn through our mistakes if we accept there is no death and we are on a transitional journey of discovery as we are born to Earth. If we do not understand what we need to learn, then we need to repeat the lesson until we do, before we are ready to move on to the next stage. When we can accept this, we free ourselves from the fear of death and know that the Self is eternal.

It is our school of learning; it is...**Earth School**.

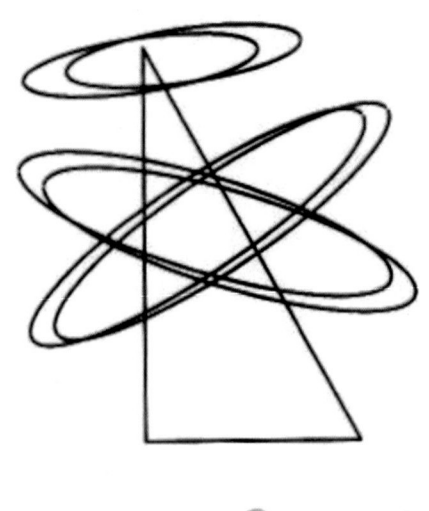